THE PROACTIVE LEADER

THE PROACTIVE LEADER

HOW TO OVERCOME PROCRASTINATION AND BE A BOLD DECISION-MAKER

DAVID DE CREMER
CHINA EUROPE INTERNATIONAL BUSINESS SCHOOL, CHINA

palgrave
macmillan

© David De Cremer 2013

All rights reserved. No reproduction, copy or transmission of this publication may be made without written permission.

No portion of this publication may be reproduced, copied or transmitted save with written permission or in accordance with the provisions of the Copyright, Designs and Patents Act 1988, or under the terms of any licence permitting limited copying issued by the Copyright Licensing Agency, Saffron House, 6–10 Kirby Street, London EC1N 8TS.

Any person who does any unauthorized act in relation to this publication may be liable to criminal prosecution and civil claims for damages.

The author has asserted his right to be identified as the author of this work in accordance with the Copyright, Designs and Patents Act 1988.

First published 2013 by
PALGRAVE MACMILLAN

Palgrave Macmillan in the UK is an imprint of Macmillan Publishers Limited, registered in England, company number 785998, of Houndmills, Basingstoke, Hampshire RG21 6XS.

Palgrave Macmillan in the US is a division of St Martin's Press LLC, 175 Fifth Avenue, New York, NY 10010.

Palgrave Macmillan is the global academic imprint of the above companies and has companies and representatives throughout the world.

Palgrave® and Macmillan® are registered trademarks in the United States, the United Kingdom, Europe and other countries.

ISBN 978-1-349-45048-0   ISBN 978-1-137-29027-4 (eBook)
DOI 10.1007/978-1-137-29027-4

This book is printed on paper suitable for recycling and made from fully managed and sustained forest sources. Logging, pulping and manufacturing processes are expected to conform to the environmental regulations of the country of origin.

A catalogue record for this book is available from the British Library.

A catalog record for this book is available from the Library of Congress.

This book is dedicated to those being close to me when making decisions that matter – my family and Jess

Contents

List of Figures and Tables ix

Chapter 1   **Introduction**   1
- Leadership and the problem of procrastination   3
- Leadership and how decisions are taken   5
- Why a democratic leader is also an autocrat   7
- The challenge   9

Chapter 2   **The psychology of the leader**   17
- Procrastination   20
- Regulating your own emotions   24
- Inaction inertia   30
- Status quo bias   33
- What are the alternatives?   37
- Neuroticism   39
- The avoidance of conflict   45
- Not being authentic   47

Chapter 3   **The psychology of the situation**   52
- Limited anonymity   53
- A climate of distrust   56
- Uncertainty   61
- Making ethical decisions   64
- The new leader   68
- The lack of previous success   72

Chapter 4   **Culture, global leadership and procrastination**   76
- Cultural dimensions and procrastination factors   77
- Culture and perceptions of time   82
- What science tells us?   83

Chapter 5   **The consequences of delaying decisions**   85
- Financial consequences   85
- Health   87
- The cost to others   89

Chapter 6   **Leader perceptions and procrastination**   92
- Positive leadership perceptions when not procrastinating   93
- Can procrastination sometimes be a good thing?   97

Chapter 7	**An interactive model**	**100**
	The 'how' of delaying decisions	102
	The 'why' of delaying decisions	105
Chapter 8	**What to do?**	**108**
	Principle 1: Never seek to justify procrastination	108
	Principle 2: Eliminate uncertainties – as far as possible	110
	Principle 3: Avoid physical and mental exhaustion	111
	Principle 4: Work at your relationships	112
	Principle 5: Be aware of the consequences of your decisions	113
Chapter 9	**The 'Leadership on Hold' – Survey©**	**115**
	Part 1: The individual	116
	I am someone who...	116
	Part 2: The context	118
	I have to make a decision in a context...	118
References		120
Index		129

List of Figures and Tables

Figures

1	Individual and contextual influences impacting irrational leadership behaviour	10
2	The onion effect caused by the individual procrastination behaviour of the leader	18
3	How to make choices between different alternatives	38
4	Social consequences of leaders' delaying decisions	90
5	An interactive model	101

Tables

1	Leadership takeaways	3
2	Summary of the impact of individual variables on the decision-making process	19
3	The use of a devil's advocate	28
4	Challenges when dealing with increased accountability as a decision-maker	56
5	The challenge of building trust	58
6	The challenges of ethical decision-making	67
7	The challenges of a new leader	69
8	Take-aways for dealing with failures	73
9	Factors affecting procrastination as a function of the salient cultural dimension	77
10	Positive leadership perceptions when not procrastinating	93
11	The bad and good of procrastination	99
12	Principles to beat procrastination	109

Chapter 1
Introduction

There is no subject about which so much has been written so often as leadership.[1] Notwithstanding the enormous number of books on this theme, there is still an air of mystique surrounding our leaders. Perhaps for this reason, the concept of leadership is still imperfectly understood, so that new and deeper perspectives are put forward at regular intervals in the hope of better explaining this key social phenomenon. Of course, relationships between people and, above all, the social dynamic that those relationships entail are by no means a simple matter. Quite the reverse, in fact. The existence of a multiplicity of theoretical analyses is therefore not necessarily a bad thing. Even when you have managed to get to grips with a social phenomenon such as leadership, it is still important to further broaden your understanding. And to help you find your way through this plethora of different viewpoints, it can do no harm to be aware that – in my opinion, at least – leadership has two dominant perspectives: the perspective of the leader and the perspective of the follower.[2]

Leadership can only exist if there are other people prepared to follow. And of course, it is not enough simply to put on a hat with the word 'leader' on it, in the hope that everyone will then accept your leadership. If people do not follow you, you will not be a leader – no matter what hat you are wearing. Followers are therefore indispensable to the concept of leadership. If you were to put Bill Clinton – one of the most charismatic and natural leader types of modern times – on a desert island, he would automatically lose his charisma and his other leadership qualities. These qualities can only exist when they are given to him by others – his followers. And the reverse is also true: followers can only exist if they have a leader figure – a person who belongs to the group but who is also sufficiently different from the others, so that he/she stands out in contrast to the background of followers.[3] The most interesting aspect of this dual perspective is that it allows the easy identification of problems relating to leadership. If both sides – the leading and the led – look at things the same way, then everything is hunky-dory! But if the leader and the followers look at something in a different way, then there is a problem. It is my conviction that by using this bifocal approach it must be possible not only to facilitate but also to optimise the flow of social and work traffic between leaders and followers – both in theoretical terms and in day-to-day practice.

In this book we will therefore use these bifocal glasses to look more closely at one of the key problems of contemporary leadership: the procrastination of leaders. If you listen carefully to the signals coming from the worlds of politics, business and finance, one of the most common complaints you will hear is that too many decisions are taken too slowly or not at all, because of the dithering behaviour of our leaders. In this context, it is important to note that the avoidance of decision-making is not the same as *laissez-faire* leadership, where more often than not the leader is simply absent.[4] No, the problem to which I refer here is the problem of leaders who either lack the necessary decisiveness and direction and thus take half-baked decisions or who simply postpone the ultimate decision that needs to be taken – in short, half-hearted leadership. The delaying of decisions in this manner is something with which we will all be familiar: from the simple postponing of your annual appraisal review to the sidelining of strategic plans and visions that were launched with such enthusiasm at the beginning of the year. For many of us, some forms of procrastination are acceptable – or at least help to make things manageable. Having said this, in many other circumstances procrastination can have serious consequences for individuals, organisations and society at large. For this reason, it is important to acquire insights into a phenomenon that has become so widespread that it even has its own special day. The French writer David d'Equainville proclaimed 26 March 2011 as 'International Procrastination Day'. A day on which everyone was allowed to take things easy and not rush into any decisions. A running joke on the Internet was, however, that the Frenchman originally scheduled this day on 25 March 2011 – completely in line with the habits of a procrastinator.

In outlining the problem of procrastination, I will highlight several key aspects of what leadership actually is all about. Put briefly, the following takeaways are essential to define leadership as it is used in this book (Table 1).

Introduction

TABLE 1 Leadership takeaways

What leadership is about

Leadership is a two-way street:

Leaders only exist when there are people who will follow. In this way, leadership is different from management as leaders have followers whereas managers have subordinates.

Followers can only be there when someone is able to lead. Being a follower implies a comparative process where the more powerful leads and the less powerful complies.

Many people like being a leader, but prefer to do this from the perspective of a follower position:

Basically, people do have a desire to be able to influence others and set directions, but only a few people are also in the game to take the risks and responsibilities associated with the job of being a leader. Thus, being formally appointed as the leader but not taking too many risks (and as we will later in this book see important decisions) is the situation that most of our leaders prefer. The heroic view of leaders taking the lead without fear has gradually disappeared in our contemporary society.

Leadership is a social process in which one individual is able to influence the others to promote the collective welfare:

This definition is used in many textbooks and points out the collective responsibilities that the one in charge carries with him or her. Nevertheless, sometimes this social burden may prove too difficult for many of our leaders, thereby instigating processes of procrastination.

Action defines the heart of leadership:

Leadership entails giving direction and guidance when striving for positive change aimed at promoting the collective welfare. In this process it is no surprise that the one in charge undertakes action to shape this change in visionary ways that appeal to the followers. In this stage, leaders take decisions that shape how they can lead by example.

At the end of the day someone has to make the decision:

Leaders define the vision that collectives pursue and motivate followers to contribute to this process. One significant and important way that leaders use to involve followers is by consulting the others. A transparent and fair decision-making process is characterised by means of giving voice to the ones being led. The problem of many contemporary leaders is that as little responsibility is taken the decision-making process is slowed down considerably. Many leaders often forget that fair decision-making also implies that after the consultation phase the one in charge actually makes a decision.

Leadership and the problem of procrastination

One of the most interesting aspects of the assertion that many leaders are prone to procrastinate is the fact that the problem is recognised by both sides of our perspective. Many leaders are well aware that the acceptance of responsibility and the taking of decisions are not getting any easier in a world that is becoming ever smaller and more complex. On the other side, followers are becoming ever-more impatient for the decisions that can bring about real change. The fact that people are happier to adopt a follower's role, so that they can more easily criticise a lack of leadership, suggests that the role of a leader is not always an enviable or desirable one. On the contrary, in our complex modern world leaders seem to be facing an increasingly Herculean task, where they are happy to accept the benefits of leadership (power and influence) but are not so keen (or able) to deal with the burden it entails (accepting responsibility and taking hard decisions). Viewed in this light, it is easier to understand the growing calls for a decentralised decision-making structure and 'leaderless teams'.[5] The basic idea seems to be to make everyone a leader, but to allow them to exercise their leadership function from within their safer role as follower.

There are numerous contemporary examples where leadership and procrastination go hand in hand. The indecisive behaviour in recent times of many of Europe's political leaders is a classic instance. The end of 2011 was marked by near chaos in the European Union, with urgent measures necessary to save the European currency. (In 2013 the danger to the euro has still not disappeared entirely.) The solutions put forward by Merkozy (het duo Merkel–Sarkozy) and the European President Herman Van Rompuy all had one thing in common: they seemed to push the problem further and further into the future. Each European summit produced another series of half-hearted (and some would say half-baked) proposals that were little more than stopgap measures, postponing a decision on the real problem to the next summit (or the one after that). All that this achieved was to give the political leaders a degree of breathing space, but they failed to use this respite to take a clear line that demonstrated the necessary will and decisiveness to tackle the crisis head on. Not surprisingly, this led to accusations of weak leadership on all sides and risked making Europe an easy prey for the sharks of the financial markets. In this respect, the Eurocrisis is indeed a textbook example of leaders who are not capable of taking the hard decisions that are so often required in difficult circumstances, which in this instance should have meant dealing with the Greece problem as quickly as possible, so that the focus could be reset on the need for all-important growth in the European economy. Commentators were quick to recall the doom scenario that devastated the Japanese economy at the beginning of the 1990s, when the Japanese leaders of the day were also blamed for taking too little action much too late, with severe consequences (low growth and a high rate of debts) that are still being felt today.

Unfortunately, the situation was not much better on the other side of the Atlantic Ocean. In the United States, President Obama was branded in 2011 as a 'weak' leader, particularly so by his Republican opponents. In the opinion of his detractors, it had become increasingly obvious that Obama displayed a tendency to prolong discussions and negotiations unnecessarily, sometimes even pointlessly, in the hope of reaching a political consensus. This idea of getting everyone 'on board' is nice in theory but is always likely to be punished in practice. It required Obama to steer an almost neutral course – in the hope of charming the majority of neutral, middle-ground voters, whose support he would need to be re-elected in 2012 – his re-election did happen and the middle-ground voters were persuaded, particularly the minority voters. But on the reverse side of the coin it made him very vulnerable to criticism that he had no clearly defined vision for the future. The signals that came out of the White House in 2011 were viewed as lacking purpose and direction, which were clear indicators of growing uncertainty. The Republicans, in particular, smelled blood at that time and did everything possible to drive the President into a corner. The fact that many crucial decisions were taken only at the very last moment illustrates that Obama's fear of being labelled as someone with strong prejudices had actually paralysed his decision-making process.

Leadership and how decisions are taken

The above examples paint a pretty poor picture of the decision-making capabilities of the Western world's current batch of political leaders. In fact, it is no exaggeration to argue that the putting off of decisions – or even an outright refusal to make them – is the most important problem in modern-day leadership.[6] This is not to say that leaders are not entitled to delay decisions for good reasons. Rather, the major problem that we nowadays face is that many of our leaders simply refrain from making a decision at all, which in a way makes them more or less invisible to the ones they are supposed to be leading.

It is vital that this problem should be recognised (and quickly), since the taking of decisions is universally regarded as a crucial element of effective leadership. Making decisions and initiating action on the basis of those decisions are part of the job description of every leader and are essential if you want to bring about change. This idea underlines the comment once made by the former US President Harry S. Truman: 'Progress occurs when courageous, skilful leaders seize the opportunity to change things for the better.' To support the noble arts of decision-making and action-taking, it is useful (and interesting) to take a look at the way leadership is described in the professional literature.

There are almost as many different definitions of leadership as there are books on the subject. However, many of these definitions have features in common and there is more or less a consensus regarding the essence of leadership: 'Leadership involves persuading other people to set aside for a period of time their individual concerns and to pursue a common goal that is important for the responsibilities and welfare of a group'.[7] This definition makes clear that leadership is a social process by which the leader – in consultation with the followers – seeks to realise and optimise the general good. As part of this process, it is important that everyone moves in the same general direction and that everyone is prepared to make a contribution towards the agreed general good. Having the power to influence people therefore also implies that the leader bears the responsibility for taking decisions; that he/she must be actively concerned with self-motivation and the motivation of others; that he/she must regularly conduct the necessary analyses that form the basis for future actions. It is this 'action' element that truly defines leadership. A lack of decisiveness and determination with regard to decision-making means by definition that such a leader cannot be an effective leader – as the above examples make abundantly clear.

For this reason, it will come as no surprise that many current theories of leadership make reference to the degree to which leaders make decisions and initiate action. The path-goal theory describes how leaders can help their 'people' – which can mean their fellow citizens, colleagues, family members and so on – to choose the right and most effective path with regard to the tasks and activities that need to be completed.[8] This most effective path presupposes a 'participative' leadership style, in which the leader consults his followers about the direction to follow. The decision process theory goes a step further and identifies the making of optimal decisions as the key task of leadership.[9] This theory makes a distinction between three styles of leadership (autocratic, collaborative and consultative) and uses seven 'yes/no' questions to determine which style is most appropriate for reaching the best decision in any given set of circumstances. The famous Ohio studies also forge a clear link with the active role played by a leader through the concept of 'initiation'.[10] Initiation assumes that the leader structures tasks and activities in such a way that it is clear which roles should be played by which people, so that the production process can operate in a smooth and coordinated manner. A further illustration of the action-oriented and decision-oriented nature of leadership can be found in the theory of transformational leadership.[11] According to Kotter, leadership is the social process that is necessary to bring about successful change for the general good.[12] Transformational types of leadership therefore have a specific focus on the ways in which a leader can shape change.[13] Leaders of this kind succeed in transforming an existing situation into a more desirable new situation.[14] This transformation process is stimulated by leaders who have a clear vision that can appeal to others, so that the leaders themselves are regarded as charismatic.[15] This requires the leaders to have a high degree of self-confidence, a willingness to make sacrifices to realise their vision and an ability to allow and accept input from their followers, in order to neutralise potential conflicts.[16]

Why a democratic leader is also an autocrat

These theories all suggest that leadership is a social process in which the leader actively sets out a pathway that can lead to an improvement of the general situation, a path that is then followed to effective realisation by the collective efforts of the group. This implies that leadership is also a visionary process, in which decisions are taken in the short-term, and not postponed indefinitely. The transformation that the resulting change ushers in is consequently active rather than passive and is motivated by a leader who is authentic and who therefore knows precisely why he/she is taking the decisions in question. This type of leader regards decisions not as an obstacle but rather as an opportunity to ensure that his/her vision and norms are translated into concrete action. Given these assumptions, it is understandable that the majority of leadership theories ascribe a key role to the elements of 'action' and 'effective decision-making'. Yet notwithstanding this clear focus, it is also important to note that most of these existing theories are prescriptive.[17] Prescription is necessary to focus on the essentials of the matter, but a purely prescriptive approach does not allow (a) a deeper investigation of the different ways in which decisions can be taken and

(b) prohibits a better understanding of how and when these different decision-making processes can be effective (or not). For this reason, there is also a need for a more descriptive approach, which will clarify the different ways in which action can be taken and which explains the processes on which that action is based. Knowing why and when people take decisions and how they transform them into concrete actions can help us to explain why many leaders have the tendency to procrastinate. This in turn implies a need to also understand the factors that can prevent people from taking action or can encourage them to do so.

This approach is similar to that adopted by Rudolph Giuliani, the former Mayor of New York City, who in his book on leadership described how fear gripped him and his team at the moment when they realised that the attack on the Twin Towers on 11 September 2011 was a terrorist attack.[18] When this kind of thing happens, people are inclined to 'freeze', so that no further decisions or action are forthcoming. However, Giuliani gave leadership a new face by realising a split-second later that action was necessary, no matter what the circumstances, and that fear was the worst possible counsellor of all. This rational control of emotions that would have paralysed most of us allowed him to coordinate rescue operations and helped him to mark out a symbolic pathway that made it possible for the New Yorkers to recover their pride and self-esteem.

The example of Mayor Giuliani demonstrates that leadership involves both a 'process' element (asking for input and evaluating it step by step) and a strong 'results' focus, which indicates what needs to be achieved. And to ensure that this end result is achieved effectively, it is necessary that people are pointed in the right direction; in other words, decisions need to be taken. When all is said and done, leadership essentially comes down to this: someone (the leader) must tell other people (the followers) what to do. Someone has to decide and others have to act. For this reason, even effective democratic leaders must sometimes behave – in part, at least – like autocrats.

Intuitively, most people will see a democratic leader as being the very opposite of an autocrat.[19] Leaders who attach the highest importance to democratic values are often portrayed as the 'ideal' leaders. However, a problem that we see to be increasing in frequency in our democratic society is that of taking effective decisions, which is becoming ever more difficult. Nowadays, being 'democratic' all too often means little more than being occupied with the process of participation. Participation is, of course, important, for a variety of reasons.

It gives us a feeling of solidarity and collective belonging; it strengthens the confidence and legitimacy of the decision-maker; and it makes the decision-making process transparent.[20] These are all explicit values that characterise a democratic leader. The problem is, however, that with the passage of time we seem to have forgotten that the point of all this participation is to ensure that a decision is finally taken.[21] And it is one of the leader's most important tasks to ensure that this actually happens! In other words, he/she must decide how to give concrete shape and form to the final outcome of the participation process. This is a heavy responsibility, but it is fundamental to the concept of leadership. In other words, a combination of democratic consultation with a hint of dictatorial decision-making is necessary if your transformation process is every really going to take off.

The challenge

In the following chapters we will look more closely at the whys and wherefores of procrastination. Having placed the problem firmly within the context of contemporary leadership, it is important to know precisely where this tendency towards indecisiveness and delay comes from. In order to map out this behaviour, it is necessary to look at both the psychological influences affecting the individual and the impact of wider circumstances on the decision-making process. Looking at both the individual tendencies that leaders – and humans in general – display and the social setting in which they have to make a decision may explain more fully why leaders can show irrational behaviour. Or put in other words, to understand that leaders' decisions become influenced by their blind spots we need to focus on how social pressures associated with the context can facilitate the elicitation of those blind spots (see Figure 1).

This interactive approach in which we zoom in on the irrational tendencies of decision-makers can be situated within the framework of the rapidly growing tradition known as 'behavioural decision-making'. The impact of this tradition is evident, for example, in the many management training courses that are now given in behavioural economics, behavioural finance and behavioural accounting.[22] All these different business activities, which were previously viewed from a purely rational perspective, are now given the label 'behavioural' to show that the previous approaches were too limited in scope and that we must pay closer attention to 'what really happens'. This tradition is also

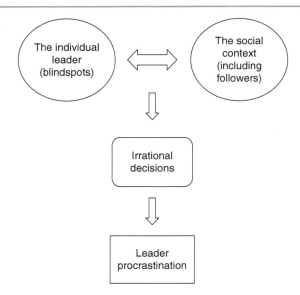

Figure 1 Individual and contextual influences impacting irrational leadership behaviour

having an increasing effect on the world's policymakers, the most striking example being the American President Obama, who makes use of behavioural economists – an area of professional expertise created by the integration of the disciplines of psychology and economy – to inspire his policy decisions.[23] The idea behind this approach is that it is no longer good enough simply to prescribe how people should make decisions. This is too normative and too rational, so that it is not realistic. It takes too little account of the fact that many decisions are anything but rational. For this reason, it is important to try and understand precisely how people take their decisions and how these insights can help us all to make better decisions of our own in the future, so that we can reduce procrastination to a minimum or even eliminate it altogether.

These insights from the behavioural tradition therefore allow us to characterise the procrastinating behaviour of leaders as irrational. This is a fundamentally different conclusion from the precept of the frequently used rational paradigm, which argues that the making of decisions in a conscious process is characterised by a way of thinking that is gradual and controlled.[24] However, many of our decisions are based on a very different kind of unconscious thinking, which is repeatedly and rapidly influenced by our routine, emotional impulses. This teaches us, for example, that people are capable of justifying their procrastination by interpreting actions and choices in a highly subjective manner, based almost exclusively on their own perceptions. In other words, personal intuition – rather than impersonal logic – is the driving force behind many of our decisions, so that our individual prejudices often play a crucial role in our decision-making process.

It is self-evident that we all display strong emotional reactions (a) when we have to do something that we don't want to do or (b) when we experience no pleasure in performing certain actions or taking certain decisions or (c) when we think that we should not be obliged to do something. If we can make the natural tendency towards procrastination comprehensible and if we can realise that a position of leadership tends to exaggerate this tendency, we will have taken important steps towards learning how to deal with this irrational behaviour. Once we know that procrastination is capable of undermining both the perceptions and actual impact of effective leadership, it is vital that we should make the problem intelligible and manageable for leaders at every level.

With this aim in mind the following chapters will contribute to our understanding of how and why leaders procrastinate in several ways. The main strengths and learning points in this book will provide the necessary input and contributions to help you to turn into a more proactive leader when it comes down to making decisions:

- The behavioural approach presented in this book will help to prove several important ideas:

    - Taking action is necessary leadership behaviour not only because it is a key element in many leadership theories but also because it is an essential ingredient influencing how followers perceive you as a leader. The absence of any decision power and willingness to make a decision invites a host of negative perceptions that can significantly undermine your leadership legitimacy and effectiveness – both in the short- and long term.
    - There is a clear difference between what leadership and management are about. Management is the minimal requirement for authority figures to do. It focuses on maintaining stability and implementing procedures. Leadership on the other hand is more than the minimum requirement. It is what makes people stand out

from others. Leadership focuses on change and the transformation processes required for implementing this change. As such, leaders have a vision that they can use as a guideline for others. Of course, guiding others in a changing world requires action on behalf of the leader.

- Despite the fact that organisations and societies become increasingly more complex, understanding the roots of leader procrastination may help to avoid being wrapped up in the web of uncertainty. Getting to understand yourself and the situation you are in can help you to make a decision, even if that decision would be to leave that situation and forego the leadership role. True leadership sometimes also involves knowing when to be the leader and when not. Regardless of your personal position, at the end of the day leadership in any form requires that action is undertaken, but with a clear mindset that makes you understand why you make those decisions.
- To recognise the idea that any form of inertia is a slowly growing kind of poison for organisations. The problem is that once you are aware of this it often is too late. For that reason, we need to educate and train leaders in proactive ways; make future leaders understand the details of the inertia process; and as such help them to recognise early signs of procrastination entering the decision-making game.

– The chapters of this book will also disprove several widely held assumptions about leadership:

- Make clear that leadership that is *too* reflective and focused on maintaining the status quo does not create momentum for change – which is an essential feature of leadership. Refraining yourself from making decisions is not the way to influence and convince followers to help building a more innovative future. Leadership by example is popular as it not only increases uncertainty about what to do but also fosters confidence and trust among the collectives that the path of action is worthwhile to pursue. Leaders being able to achieve that kind of state will be able to lead and move forward.
- Leaders who delay decisions do not promote cohesion and social affiliations within organisations and societies. Rather they create

feelings of uncertainty, bringing to the fore a lack of identity and vision. As a result, collectives may actually become more fragmented when leaders do not take action and make decisions. In fact, leadership that remains with the status quo in a way does not signal that the leader is one with the existing collective; it rather signals that his or her role is limited for the welfare and functioning of that collective.

- Leadership is not only about the individual! It is primarily about being able to manage and connect with others. Leadership is not a personal concept; it is a social concept. Making a decision implies not only which action will be taken but also which action(s) will not be taken. This very fact illustrates that leaders need to have abilities to foster harmony in times when tough decisions need to be made and not all followers can be satisfied in their choices. At such moments, leaders need to possess the necessary social skills to manage relationships and the necessary awareness to be able to outline the consequences of procrastination.

- Active leadership is required not only when confronted with problems. Specifically, many contemporary leaders hold the idea that they only have to think about making decisions when problems actually arise. This is not the way to go! The ideal way is, of course, to prevent problems, and if this is not possible then he/she should be able to display effective damage control measures. Being able to engage in effectively managing problems and failures requires that one, at least, has the knowledge why those failures in the first place emerge. With respect to leadership this suggests that one gathers the necessary insights into why one may procrastinate and fail to address underlying problems. Moreover, being able to increase one's insights and sense of awareness with respect to procrastination already helps you to develop into a proactive leader. In light of this approach, a proactive leadership style is therefore by definition the type of leadership that emphasises the action element. Taking action and making decisions by definition includes the refusal of hesitation and delaying leadership styles.

An important question that you as a leader will have to address is 'why it is necessary to get a deeper understanding of procrastination in the leadership arena?' What are the compelling reasons that make leaders delay decisions and that one should be aware of?

- Knowing yourself with respect to how you make decisions makes you in a way already a more effective leader. It enables you to be more hands-on and to anticipate pitfalls in your environment. This type of skill will allow you to make decisions even when others are not yet thinking about the next step. This again outlines the potential of a proactive leadership style: you will not only avoid increasing complexities in your environment and invite problems to blossom but you will also be ahead of the competition in many ways! This proactive focus will facilitate the development of your agenda and help decide what is important to focus on now and in the future.

- Understanding why you may delay decisions to the extent that others will get frustrated will help you to recognise your blind spots when it comes down to decision-making. As noted earlier, as human beings we like to think we are in control and are able to act in rational ways whenever the pressure is on. Reality, however, is that we are more often biased in our judgements and hence decisions than we realise. Being able to identify at least some of your blind spots will help you to become better equipped in accurately evaluating the necessity of which decisions have to be made and which ones can be delayed. A more realistic approach to decision-making is promoted by insights into your human behaviour.

- Focusing on the negative consequences that leader procrastination may reveal for followers and the larger society highlights the notion that leadership is all about interdependencies. As a leader your decisions influence the outcomes and welfare of others. Too often decisions are analysed in isolated ways in which the social consequences are underestimated. And even if those social consequences are taken into account they more often than not make leaders refrain from making a decision, thereby being blind to the idea that not making a decision at all may harm others even more.

- Refraining from the decision-making process as a leader reduces the extent to which one is able to exert influence. Leadership is about using your influence to get things moving in responsible and visionary ways. Not making decisions turns your leadership not into a visible and appealing strategy but rather into an invisible position within the organisation. By definition, being in a leadership position makes you visible and invites responsibility by engaging in active and constructive efforts. From that point of view, invisible leadership cannot be related to responsibility-taking.

- Recognising the pivotal role of decision-making in your leadership should make you more aware of the extent to which people are averse to uncertainty. Understanding that uncertainty undermines productivity, performance and commitment of followers, you will quickly realise that delaying decisions is not an option. It only adds to the feeling of uncertainty that people experience. As a leader you have to create meaning to the ones you are leading and this requires being clear and to the point. Any acts that increase the level of uncertainty reduce meaning within the organisation, making followers feel less loyal.

Finally, the insights promoted in this book will not only be fruitful to you in terms of developing a conceptual understanding of the problem but also help you grow into a leadership position in which you feel confident and effective, because of the following advantages:

- You will make decisions that remain more close to the values and ideals that you stand for. In this respect, making decisions in an active and conscious way will not only make you feel more authentic but also make followers perceive you as being authentic.
- It will allow you to motivate people in active ways. By taking decisions you lead by example and feed directly into the motivation of followers by offering them guidance. This way you prevent your followers from getting stuck in the mindset of a procrastinator themselves.
- Your leadership style will provide meaning to the organisation in what they stand for and what the goals should be to pursue. Being able to make decisions will not add further layers of complexity but instead will reduce it.
- It will define who you are as a leader. Specifically, being aware of the decision-making dilemma (doing something versus nothing) will motivate you to focus on your area of expertise in which you are more at ease to take up responsibilities. This process will

produce a more effective leadership style that allows you to truly exert influence on your followers.

- It will help you to understand when it is time for a new formal leadership to enter. Being the leader is not a job that is forever. Depending on the specific situation or the specific expertise required, different leaders may come to the fore. Your strength will be to recognise whether the decisions and actions that are required fit your profile or not. If it does you will thrive with passion and confidence. If it does not then it will alert you that it is better to look for coalitions or a replacement. Being able to do this in an appropriate manner will add legitimacy to your informal leadership.

Chapter 2
The psychology of the leader

In these tempestuous times, it should hardly be necessary to underline the need for leaders to accept responsibility and act decisively. However, it is disappointing to conclude that this is not happening. Many important decisions are not being taken with the level of resoluteness that is necessary. Quite the contrary, all too often, key decisions are being postponed and many political and business leaders seem reluctant to cut to the heart of difficult problems. The procrastination of their leaders is one of the most frustrating aspects reported by employees at all levels and in all sectors. Most readers will be familiar with situations where important matters have been 'put on the back burner', so that no change was implemented and no progress booked. Moreover, it seems to be a problem that has gotten worse in recent years, so that we now find ourselves in a situation that can be compared to an onion, with successive layers of delayed decisions gradually being superimposed, one on top of the other. This obviously makes it even more difficult to take the corrective action that is now required. In fact, because different layers of imperfect decision-making emerge, the level of complexity within the organisation will increase dramatically. Therefore, the *onion-effect* is in danger of paralysing the entire decision-making apparatus from top to bottom (see Figure 2).

It has been shown statistically that organisations with effective leaders are (on average) thirteen times more likely than companies with ineffective leaders to perform well financially, to offer better goods and services and to create greater satisfaction with both employees and customers. In other words, it is blindingly obvious that the procrastinating behaviour of our leaders is damaging to the collective good. For this reason alone, it is crucial to gain further insights into the nature of the problem. In passing, it is interesting to note that the indisputable existence of procrastination stands in sharp contrast to the traditional image of leaders as action-driven people, with a clear vision and a clear plan for its implementation. We expect our leaders to be decision-hungry, not decision-shy – and this is not an unreasonable

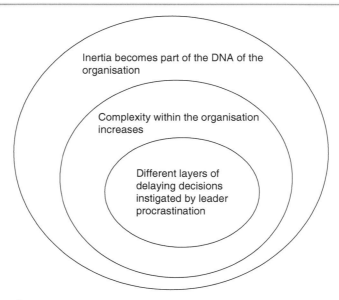

Figure 2 The onion effect caused by the individual procrastination behaviour of the leader

expectation. Particularly in times of crisis – as in the current European financial crisis – it is irresponsible of leaders to continually postpone key decisions. The longer our leaders dither, the narrower the window of opportunity becomes to take effective reforms that might actually lead us out of the mess in which we find ourselves.

Making decisions and implementing action in times of crisis is therefore an important part of leadership. As soon as the need for a decision arises, it is assumed that a leader will not only formulate an objective but also draw up a plan that will see this vision carried through into positive action. As part of this process, it is also rationally assumed that the leader will possess the skills and competencies necessary to make the decisions required. In terms of this rational approach, a responsible leader is therefore a leader that takes decisions. However, the lessons of behavioural economics and psychology indicate that people do not always react in a rational manner, particularly in situations where there is a degree of uncertainty or where time pressure is involved. In these circumstances – circumstances where it is often necessary to make a decision – our behaviour is much more likely to be influenced by irrational tendencies. It is almost as if these tendencies allow us to deceive ourselves into believing that we are behaving objectively, whereas in

The psychology of the leader

reality we are behaving subjectively. Research has shown that self-deception of this kind is present in many different fields of human activity. For example, the majority of people honestly believe that they are better than average drivers – which, of course, is a statistical impossibility. The same over-optimistic tendency is observable in people who are asked to estimate the time necessary to complete a task or make a decision. The majority allow themselves too little time to complete a task and too much time to take a decision – often much more than the situation warrants. Few people see the need for immediate decisions. It is therefore important that we should seek to map and analyse the irrational factors that can be linked to this tendency to put off decisions or behave hesitantly.

For this reason, in this chapter we will look more closely at the person and personality of the leader, and at the individual psychological impulses that can help to limit harmful procrastination. Specifically, we will zoom in more closely on the individual factors that have not been recognised much in the past and that actually make leaders slow down decision-making in such a way that plans and strategies are not fully implemented, leading to irrational behaviour on the part of the leader and increased complexity on the part of the organisation. In Table 2

TABLE 2 Summary of the impact of individual variables on the decision-making process

General Idea:
Leaders develop visions and implement those in rational ways
Leaders have the necessary skills and competencies to do so
Leaders engage in a rational strategy of decision-making

Variables promoting irrationality in the decision-making process:
- Procrastination
- Difficulties in regulation of your own emotions
- Suffering from inaction inertia
- Promoting status quo thinking
- Evaluating alternatives in inefficient ways
- Developing a neurotic leadership style
- Avoiding conflicts
- Not being authentic

Outcome of the irrational decision-making process:
- Decisions are delayed throughout the organisation
- Complexity increases and inertia becomes the second nature of the organisation

I briefly summarise the individual variables that will be discussed in this chapter.

Procrastination

Procrastination is a term used in the professional literature to indicate the postponing of decisions and actions. This concept has received growing attention in recent times, since the amount of procrastination has increased systematically during the last 40 years.[25] This is confirmed by the fact that 20% of the world's population now describe themselves as procrastinators.[26] The consequences of this increase are not inconsiderable (as will be explained in Chapter 5). It is a concept that is familiar to many of us, since it crops up everywhere in our lives. Are you going to pay that bill on time or are you going to leave it to the end of the month? And what about filling in your tax return? Surely that can wait until next week? And it doesn't always work to your advantage. Have you ever delayed using a gift voucher until it passes its expiry date? Or left all your Christmas shopping to the very last minute? Procrastination therefore involves postponing important matters and pushing them to the long term, while you deal with much less important matters in the short term. It is characteristic of people who are particularly prone to procrastination to actively go in search of distractions that can assist their 'habit'. And the easier or more accessible the distraction is, the better. The constant checking of e-mails is a favourite distraction of this kind. Are you going to write that difficult report? 'Later, perhaps. I've got 20 mails I need to look at first...'

There are three criteria that allow us to define behaviour as procrastination.[27] The first is that the behaviour makes people less efficient. The second is performing tasks that are not necessary to ensure the good execution of more important tasks. In other words, the behaviour is unnecessary. Finally, the behaviour delays the implementation of important tasks. Viewed from this perspective, it should be clear that procrastination is an irrational form of behaviour. It is behaviour that you adopt voluntarily, while at the same time being aware that the behaviour will probably lead to poorer results.[28] Procrastination therefore means that the person concerned initially had the intention to make a decision or take action, but ultimately displays behaviour that negates that intention.[29] In other words, procrastination is actually a kind of sabotage that people perpetrate against themselves by putting off crucial decisions or action. This creates more uncertainty, by allowing the problem to drag on and by refusing to take the necessary remedial steps to stop the escalation of indecision. In this sense, it is also predictable that procrastination will eventually lead to a situation that can no longer be put right. If you dither and delay for too long, you will one day find that there is no way back. The return path is blocked. For this reason, it is very important that we should be aware of the need to take timely action, so that our lack of decisiveness does not lead to our isolation and immobilisation.

But is this as easy as it sounds? Are our leaders capable of stopping and even reversing this escalation of inaction? All too often, we see people develop the tendency to procrastinate with apparent effortlessness. Once you have done it once or twice, it gets easier and easier – but also harder to stop. This, of course, is the real danger. Leaders who continually postpone decisions become tangled in a web of their own making, where one moment of indecisiveness almost automatically leads to the next one, so that inaction becomes the rule rather than the exception. How can you possibly justify this to yourself? This, too, can be quite easy. Many procrastinating leaders are masters of self-deception. They are experts at finding dozens of plausible sounding reasons to explain why they are doing nothing. Why, in fact, it is actually beneficial to do nothing! As we have mentioned earlier, it is important for people to have a positive image of themselves. This means that many of our self-justificatory explanations are based on what we would like to believe rather than on the realities of the situation. The manner in which we assess ourselves to be honest, competent and motivated people is seldom accurate. We often overestimate our abilities in these dimensions, so that at first we fail to realise that we are capable of harmful behaviour, such as procrastination. Some of the 'reasons' most commonly used by procrastinators include the following:

- I work better under pressure;
- This is not all that important; I'll deal with it later;
- Pressure makes me more creative;
- I am someone who knows their own abilities and boundaries, so I know that there is still plenty of time to do this tomorrow, or the next day.

This last example is both typical and illuminating. Procrastination is often related to an incorrect assessment of time. We are all occasionally guilty of thinking that we have more than enough time, whereas in reality we have no time at all. Because we think that we are competent, we believe that time is less of a problem for us than it is for other people. Research has shown that there is indeed a clear relationship between time and procrastination. However, this relationship has little to do with our ability to predict accurately or inaccurately how quickly time passes. Instead, the problem is related to our subjective (as opposed to objective) experience of time. In essence, time is an objective given. It can be measured. Yet notwithstanding this objective truth, people can still experience the passage of time differently. For some it goes quickly, for others more slowly.[30]

This distinction between the objective and subjective experience of time is relevant for understanding why different people also display different levels of procrastination. Studies have concluded, for example, that a subjective experience of time plays an important role in determining whether or not people are capable of delaying the collection of a promised reward.[31] In a similar manner, the problem of procrastination is more prevalent in people who tend to underestimate the amount of time necessary to complete a task satisfactorily. People are by nature optimistic when it comes to believing that everything will be ready on time. This is because we take too little account of potential distractions when assessing how much time we need. In other words, we are deceiving ourselves again. We are competent and so we know exactly how to deal with the problem in hand. What can possibly go wrong? Well, quite a lot actually. And when it does, our time calculations immediately come under pressure – and so we postpone and delay.

This tendency to overestimate ourselves and underestimate the time we need is sometimes referred to as the 'planning fallacy'.[32] We have already mentioned it before: nearly everyone submits their tax return at the very last minute, even though we received the form months ago and swore to ourselves that this year we would be on time. And the same phenomenon is also evident at all levels of society. How often do we see that political measures, which in theory are relatively simple to implement, are postponed for so long that they lose their effect or are never even implemented at all? In short, we all have a strong tendency to underestimate the time we need to complete a task successfully. And it is important to note that this tendency persists, irrespective of the amount of experience you have acquired. In fact, the greater your experience, the greater your tendency to underestimate becomes, so that

The psychology of the leader

your level of procrastinating behaviour increases. Belief in your own tried-and-tested abilities makes you inclined to opt for the most optimistic scenario: after all, you have been doing this job for years! It is a kind of wishful thinking that persuades you to reach the subjective targets you have set inside your own head, rather than focusing on the objectivities of the situation.[33]

In view of these potential pitfalls, it is important to know which insights can help us to prevent procrastination from becoming a habit, a habit that we will otherwise find extremely difficult to break. The more we keep on postponing something, the harder it becomes to take a decision relating to that something. And even if you do finally take a decision, after delaying too long, there is always a chance that it will be the wrong decision, so that your indecisiveness and its negative consequences will quickly become apparent to everyone. This type of situation is very damaging to your reputation as a leader and is something that you should seek to avoid at all costs. Worse still, it breeds a kind of fear for making decisions, so that on the next occasion you are required to make a tough call, you are even more inclined to procrastinate. To escape the possibility of being trapped in this escalating downward spiral, it is crucial that leaders should exercise a high degree of self-control. Self-control at the emotional, physical and strategic levels. This requires the leader to map out in advance precisely what objectives he/she wishes to achieve, so that possible distractions that may lead to time pressure can be identified – and counteracted.

To summarise, fighting procrastination in ways that you regain self-control implies that leaders are clear about the WHAT they want to pursue and HOW they will do this. The WHAT refers to the vision that the leader in agreement with the organisation develops. The HOW refers to the direction the leader chooses to implement the vision. In developing the HOW-part of the decision-making process it is important for the leader to stay in control at the – already mentioned – three levels: emotional, physical and strategic.

Emotional level

- Deal with your negative emotions
- Try to put every step you take in perspective

Physical level

- Get energy from the things you find pleasure in
- Be passionate about what you do
- Anticipate the pitfalls you may encounter and remove them where possible from the direction you have chosen

Strategic level

- Know your weaknesses and strengths
- Pick your battles – only the ones important to the implementation of your vision matter
- Remain loyal to the coalitions and relationships that you need the most and foster their long-term survival

Regulating your own emotions

A whole range of negative emotions are often associated with postponed decisions. These are not only the emotions we experience during the moment itself but also the emotions we expect to feel whenever a decision is made. These latter emotions are known as *anticipated emotions*. Because of the existence of these anticipated emotions, leaders can sometimes be stimulated to postpone a decision or even avoid making it altogether. For example, leaders frequently assume that by making the decision they will cause something to happen that will have negative consequences for themselves. This fear of regret can lead them to delay the decision, often indefinitely.[34]

Most forms of procrastination are related to some extent with fear. This fear can be linked to many different potential consequences, such as a loss of reputation or the loss of future opportunities. In other words, fear would seem to be a bad counsellor for a decision-maker. Because the fear we feel comes from within ourselves and because our emotional life is not fully objective, we will overestimate the importance of these emotions and will allow ourselves to be influenced by them, even though we know that this is not the most 'rational' course of action. Because we experience our emotions in a very personal manner, we are more inclined to believe what they tell us, which can lead to irrational behaviour, such as the postponing of decisions.

This means that decision-makers need a certain degree of control over their emotions and a good understanding of how they work. The ability to regulate your emotions is a skill that can help you to take positive and timely decisions, rather than postponing them to some undefined point in the future. In fact, one of the major differences between decisive and indecisive people is precisely the extent to which they are able to interpret and deal effectively with their own emotions. In the professional literature, people capable of good emotional regulation are said to have a strong action orientation.[35] People with a strong action orientation can cope with negative emotions in a controlled manner. They have the ability to rapidly analyse and assess their feelings of fear, so that they can give them a proper place in their thinking. In this way, their negative emotions are not left hanging, so that they cannot exercise a limiting effect on the decision-making process. Research has confirmed that a strong action orientation will help you to persist longer in your attempts to reach a specific objective, even though this might involve high levels of exhaustion and stress.[36] On the reverse side of the coin, if you are not able to control your negative emotions, you will remain in a negative frame of mind, which can only increase your feelings of doubt and apprehension, so that you will be less and less inclined to take a decision.

What factors determine whether or not a person is good at regulating their emotions? Studies have shown that people who possess a positive self-image that is strongly related to their own emotional experiences are better able to control negative feelings, both implicitly and explicitly. People with a strong action orientation are able to activate this positive self-image whenever they are confronted with their own negative emotions. It is almost as if they have a kind of automatic pilot. If there is a strong association between your emotions and your self-image, you will be capable of neutralising your negative emotions quickly and effectively, so that you will be in a better position to take positive action.[37] People who do not have a strong action orientation generally display a weak correlation between their self-image and the emotions they experience.[38] This means that their negative emotions often remain unresolved, so that they can exercise their negative effect on their decisions.[39] Consequently, this reasoning demonstrates why it is important that people should develop a positive attitude towards themselves. This in turn suggests that leaders should seek out positive experiences, so that they can develop a more positive self-image, which they can then relate to their emotional experience. In other words, it is possible to create a kind of buffer – your positive self-image – that can block out and neutralise your feelings of negativity. It is important that you should be aware of this fact, since research has proven that this relationship works at an unconscious level, so that it is not explicitly under your control.

It is equally important to note that the activation of a positive self-image – that can act as a buffer against your negative anticipated emotions – is linked to the extent to which you are able to regulate yourself. But what does this mean exactly? In order to control your own emotions, it is first necessary to control your own impulses and motivators. If you are too impulsive, it will be difficult to regulate your emotions and your self-image. And observations do indeed show that impulsive people are also the people most likely to postpone or defer decisions. If you are impulsive, you are much more inclined to shoot off at odd tangents, jumping from one emotional extreme to the other. Being impulsive means that your lack of self-control will allow you to devote too much attention to distractions that have nothing to do with the task in hand. Impulsive people like to be occupied with several different things at the same time. By being involved with 'everything' in this manner, they create a false feeling of control. The more things they have on their plate, the more 'meaningful' their life becomes. This is a dangerous piece of self-deception. Too much impulsiveness can be fatal for leaders. By definition, leadership means maintaining a clear focus on the collective welfare of the group, whereas impulsive people are often poorly understood by others – and vice versa. This leads to uncertain and unpredictable situations, which can seriously undermine the leader's willingness to be decisive.

In order to suppress your impulses, you therefore need a high level of self-control. A lack of self-control can have serious negative consequences for your ability to function effectively. It encourages negative characteristics, such as aggressive feelings, obsessive thoughts, health problems and depression.[40] It is also damaging for your social functioning as a leader. For example, it may make you less inclined to be helpful and more inclined to breach certain ethical norms.[41,42]

How can you sharpen your self-control? A general rule is that you must take good care of yourself in all areas of your life. This means that you need to seek calm and simplicity, both physical and mental. Leaders need self-control to find the discipline necessary to make the decisions that need to be made. For this reason, it is important that leaders should get enough sleep, that they are not exposed to all kinds of irrelevant distractions and that they are not subjected to excessive stress (see Chapter 6).[43] Very recent research suggests that self-control can be fed and nourished. Studies by Baumeister and Tierney indicate that people show greater determination if they are fed sugar.[44] In other words, sugar increases self-control. The researchers showed that test subjects who drank a milkshake between two difficult and energy-consuming tasks were able to continue working with greater enthusiasm than a second group of test subjects who drank low-calorie yoghurt between the two tasks. In other words, the higher calorie intake increased the willpower of the milkshake drinkers and made them better able to control their behaviour. The researchers do, however, point out that in non-laboratory conditions it is probably better to take on added protein rather than added sugar. 'Get some healthy food into your body, wait an hour, and then the decision won't seem so overwhelming' (p. 247).

A final important point is that leaders must develop the ability to distinguish between major matters and minor matters. Because of their position of authority, leaders are frequently presented with opportunities to surrender to their impulses. For this reason, it is important that leaders should have trustworthy confidants and advisers, who can point out and (hopefully) limit their leader's impulsive behaviour. In particular, they should try to filter out the number of distractions to which the leader is subject. This means that mechanisms must exist which allow and encourage the leader to delegate, so that he/she is only confronted with the most crucial decisions, the ones that really need his/her attention.[45] These advisory 'deputies' therefore perform a very important task: by helping the leader to sort the relevant from the irrelevant, they ensure continued focus on the key task(s). The famous story of the Trojan horse is a brilliant example of this phenomenon at work.

In his excellent book about procrastination (pp. 185–186), Piers Steel points to the relevance of this story, as recounted in the epic work *The Odyssey,* written over 3000 years ago by the Greek poet Homer.[46] Odysseus was the king of Ithaca. He left his kingdom to take part in the war against Troy, one of whose princes had run off with the beautiful Helen, daughter of the Greek king. To capture Troy and recover Helen, the Greeks devised a cunning plan, which involved a hollow wooden horse. They left the horse – seemingly a gift but actually packed full of Greek soldiers – outside the city walls. When the Trojans took their 'prize' into the city, the soldiers sprang out, opened the city gates from the inside and let in the waiting army of Odysseus and his comrades. The trick worked and Troy fell. During his journey home to Ithaca, Odysseus became involved in all kinds of dangerous adventures with monsters, giants and even with sirens: beautiful women of the sea whose equally beautiful sing lured sailors to their doom on the rocks. Fortunately for Odysseus, he had met and charmed the goddess Circe, who advised him to stop the ears of his crew with beeswax, so that they could not hear the signing, while he was tied to the mast of his ship, so that he could not give way to his impulses when he heard the heavenly voices. This clever tactic worked, and Odysseus reached home in safety.

In other words, the captain of the ship was able to resist the sirens because the crew had tied him to the mast. In this way, it was impossible for him to behave impulsively. This ancient story therefore shows that we all need a *devil's advocate,* someone who can point out our impulses as soon as they arise and help us to resist them (see Table 3). The effect is even more beneficial if it is possible to agree on some form

---

TABLE 3 The use of a devil's advocate

Why pick a devil's advocate?

- This person will provide you with a different perspective than the one that you are using when having to make a decision. Human beings are self-serving in many areas of life and this greatly influences how we interpret and evaluate situations. That is, we tend to look at events taking place mostly from only our own perspective, without taking into account the desires of others and how this may influence how they look at the same situation.
- This person may help you to become more realistic in how to evaluate yourself as a decision-maker. Human beings are very strongly motivated to achieve very positive self-presentations. This results in many of us suffering from an enhanced self-view that makes us miss important details when making decisions that involve ourselves.

Where to get one?

- Always look for two different types of devil's advocates. One who is not part of your business life – and therefore has no shared interest whether your decisions will affect your business – and one who is part of your business environment. You will learn the most by looking for the discrepancies in opinions of those two people. If discrepancies emerge between the two of them, then you should be aware that it is a situation where procrastination may hit hard.
- Look in your circle of trust, but make sure that you pick someone who is willing to deliver some criticism. Often trust is highest in people who are close to you, but the mere fact that those people would criticise you is also frightening. On the other hand, being criticised by someone you trust will enhance the likelihood that you will use this feedback in constructive ways.

of pre-commitment, which allows impulses to be anticipated. But this is not always easy, since impulses are by their very nature irrational, and consequently difficult to predict. Because we are so governed by our emotions, we are often blind to them. Leaders also have these blind spots, and for this reason they need a confederate who can help them to open their eyes – and prevent them from making a fool of themselves.

> ### Examples of leaders regulating emotions and making decisions
>
> #### Rudolph Giuliani
>
> Rudolph Giuliani is an American lawyer, who served as Mayor of New York City (NYC) from 1994 to 2001. He is known for being very decisive and knowing what he wants. This is reflected nicely in two important achievements. The first achievement is the fact that he was able to reduce the crime rate significantly in NYC and as such contributed strongly to the quality of life of the NY citizens. He did this in a controlled and tough manner, in which he was able to strike a balance between ratio and emotion. The second important achievement concerns his leadership role after the attack on the World trade Center on 11 September 2001, which gained him international recognition.
>
> His leadership at that moment is often used as the prime example of someone stepping up and leading the city out of chaos. Giuliani was credited for having the ability to stay calm and make thoughtful and controlled decisions, while being under immense pressure. For that reason, Time Magazine named him Person of the Year and concluded that he could be self-righteous, but always in (emotional) control, ensuring that he gets things done.[47]
>
> #### Boris Johnson
>
> He is a member of the British Conservative party and most known as the elected Mayor of London since 2008. He is infamous for making comments without hesitation and being fuelled by clear emotional flavours. For example, in 2001, he was very critical about the issue of gay marriage – a position he played down considerably in recent years. For that reason, he has been criticised often as not being serious enough to be Mayor and overly emotional and impulsive, making him appear insincere and – as Ken Livingstone noted – even can be seen as a 'joke'.

(Continued)

> In recent years, Johnson seems to be less of loose cannon and has learned to regulate his emotions in a better way by playing down some of his aversions and impulses, making his decision-making strategies more coherent and being less plagued by a loss of attention to the topic. Some may even say that his decisions even carry some vision with it nowadays.

Inaction inertia

It is important for leaders to assess the impact of their own emotions and to learn how to deal with this impact. Good regulation of your emotions will help you to avoid procrastinating behaviour (most of the time, at least). However, it is equally necessary for leaders to understand that this regulatory process relates not only to the emotions that you expect to feel but also to the impact of emotions that you have already experienced in the past. Failure to do this explains, for example, why leaders frequently make decisions that are incomprehensible to the outside world. Even though it is sometimes obvious to everyone else what decision needs to be taken, our leaders seem to be deaf to reason and blind to the objective facts that are staring them in the face. It is almost as if they make a deliberate choice to avoid the most rational decision.

A good example of this is the phenomenon whereby leaders, once they have missed a good opportunity, are inclined to make the same mistake when a new opportunity arises in the future. This second opportunity may be highly advantageous in its own right, but because it is less beneficial than the first opportunity that has been missed, the leaders are often reluctant to seize their new chance. They are hesitant and avoid taking action – so that the new opportunity also slips by. Viewed from a distance, people will often say that the behaviour of leaders in these circumstances is not logical. If an opportunity is in your interests and can increase your well-being, why on earth should you refuse to consider it? The problem is that the second opportunity activates a kind of reverse thinking, which persuades (or deceives) leaders into believing that the reality of the past situation could have been different. In other words, it could and should have been possible to exploit the first opportunity. This type of thinking is known as 'counterfactual thinking', when a leader ignores the real facts and becomes convinced that a different outcome could have been achieved. The leader begins to imagine what it would have felt like if this first opportunity had been successfully concluded. And because this first opportunity was potentially more beneficial than the second one, but was not taken, this induces such strong emotions in the leader that he/she refuses to contemplate the new opportunity or delays, taking the required action for so long that the opportunity once again passes. In other words, the second opportunity underlines just how advantageous the first opportunity really was. This leads to feelings of regret and frustration in the decision-maker, which also paralyses his/her ability to act second time around.

Expressed differently, this means that leaders anticipate the regret that they will feel at the moment when they accept the second – less attractive – opportunity. If only they had taken that golden first opportunity, when they had the chance! The consequences of such thinking are not difficult to imagine. No decision is taken and the second opportunity is also lost. Yet avoiding a decision in this manner is wholly irrational. It has negative effects not only for the leader but also for the group he/she leads. Moreover, it can lead to a succession of poor decisions (or non-decisions), a process of escalation that can sometimes be very difficult to break and is often damaging for the long-term general good. The poor management of decision-making, caused by the poor management of personal emotions, can therefore have far-reaching consequences for the future.

This phenomenon of not taking a decision when you have missed a similar but better opportunity in the past is known in the literature as 'inaction inertia'.[48] The strong desire of people to avoid negative emotions – in particular, the emotion of regret – with regard to things that they have not been able to achieve in the past means that many leaders become incapable of taking action or making decisions when a new opportunity arises, which is less lucrative than a previously missed opportunity, but is nonetheless still beneficial to the welfare of the group that the leader represents. It is self-evident that leaders who employ this irrational decision-making strategy will regularly find themselves in situations where everyone loses – themselves most of all.

An inherent aspect of this debilitating strategy is that leaders behave negatively – by failing to take the right decisions – in order to avoid short-term feelings of regret. Yet in the long-term, this can lead to even greater negative consequences that can usually be predicted in advance.[49] What most leaders fail to realise is that when the long-term consequences of inaction finally become apparent, the feelings of regret will be much deeper and much longer lasting than the feelings of regret they initially wanted to avoid in the short term. At this moment, they will understand that the regret you feel at not taking a decision is much harder to bear than the regret you feel if you have at least taken some action. In other words, it is better to have tried and failed than not to have tried at all. The avoidance of decisions for reasons of anticipated regret is therefore irrational, because it means that leaders not only miss out on beneficial opportunities in the short term but also make things much more difficult for themselves and their group in the long term. This avoidance behaviour also means that the leader and, by extension, the organisation fail to receive corrective feedback, which strangles the learning potential that is necessary to encourage the innovative ideas that one expects from visionary leaders. For this reason, it is therefore important, when leaders are inclined to yield to the temptation of anticipated regret that someone is on hand to make them aware of both the short-term *and* the long-term consequences of their behaviour. This can best be achieved through a system of transparent leadership, where the group can contribute input to the decision-making process.

This strategy is very similar to the strategy described by Herodotus in his *Histories,* written 450 years before the birth of Christ: 'If an important decision is to be made [the Persians] first discuss the question when they are drunk. The following day the master of the house...submits their decision for reconsideration when they are sober. If they still approve, it is adopted; if not, it is abandoned. Conversely, any decision they make when they are sober is reconsidered afterwards, when they are drunk.' If the short-term avoidance of regret is equivalent to being drunk, then it is possible to regard a more long-term perspective as the equivalent of being sober. Leaders should be in a position to make use of both perspectives, in order to reach balanced, timely and well-considered decisions.

To ensure that well-considered decisions are ultimately taken, remember:

(i) Taking action is better than not trying at all
(ii) Not to miss out on any corrective feedback and opportunities for innovation
(iii) To use both pro- and contra-arguments for evaluating a deal or decision

Status quo bias

We are all familiar with the so-called decision dilemma. Things do not turn out as planned and we suddenly find ourselves in an unexpected crisis. What should we do? Stick to our original strategy or change our way of thinking, to avoid similar problems in the future? The rational decision-maker in each of us realises that adjusting the current situation to reflect new circumstances represents what would generally be regarded as a responsible correction. You initiate and support a transformation process which amends the present situation in a way that will allow you to prevent a comparable problem from arising in the future. Yet notwithstanding the fact that many crises are caused by error or omissions, many leaders are reluctant to implement corrections of this kind. Their fear for the unknown persuades them to leave everything 'as it is'. This flawed way of thinking is known in the professional literature as the 'status quo bias'.[50]

The status quo bias means that we are more inclined to preserve an existing state of affairs than we are to change it. However, at certain moments – during times of crisis in particular – it becomes evident that change is urgent and inevitable. The financial crisis of 2008 gave an unmistakably clear signal that fundamental weaknesses had crept into our financial system, both at an individual and at an institutional level. However, the emergence of the Eurocrisis in 2011–2012 – which was largely a result of the 2008 banking crisis – made painfully clear that very little has so far changed (not only in terms of increased regulation, but also in terms of the mindset of the bankers themselves). It seems that all those involved – politicians and financiers alike – had a preference for leaving things 'untouched'. This is flying in the face of reason. If we know that an existing situation led to a crisis in the past and might possibly lead to a similar crisis in the future, it is only logical to conclude that the situation must be changed. Even so, Europe's most powerful leaders are apparently more comfortable with the feel of the known than with the fear of the unknown. And as a result of their fear, they avoid taking the decisions that need to be taken.

The status quo bias is particularly evident in negotiations, above all when the negotiators fail to create any added value. If they are unable to increase what is on the table – 'enlarging the pie' as it is known – then all that remains is to redistribute what was already on offer. In other words, simply holding on to what you have already got works against the potentially beneficial forces of change – and therefore leads to disappointing results for all concerned. This demonstrates that the status quo bias has a powerful effect on our thinking. But why exactly?

Our human nature tells us that we should always try to give or pay as little as possible in all dimensions of our life. The desire to avoid cost expresses itself in behaviour that attempts to avoid irritating, negative emotions, such as fear and insecurity. The existing situation – what we have – is already known to us. In spite of the flaws that we know it contains, we feel comfortable with this situation; it holds no fears for us. But it is different with a new and unfamiliar situation. This represents a step into the unknown – and unknown, as the old saying puts it, is unloved. For this reason, voluntarily opting to accept a new situation will only occur if the new situation is highly attractive. Unfortunately, this is often not the case (differences in 'attractiveness' can be very subtle), so that most of us hang on to what we have already got – which merely serves to increase the likelihood of a new crisis in the not-too-distant future. Moreover, the greater the number of alternative choices, the stronger the status quo bias becomes. Leaders who must manage a crisis in which there are plenty of different options for action often tend to freeze: the complexity of the different alternatives and the fear of what they might represent make it 'safer' and 'easier' to do nothing. 'Je maintiendrai', as the motto of the House of Orange puts it: 'What I have, I hold.' The more difficult the decision – perhaps because of a multiplicity of options or the importance of the occasion – the stronger the inclination towards inaction. 'Let sleeping dogs lie,' to coin another old adage.

The strong presence of this bias suggests that in general people find it easier to do nothing. But this is not the kind of behaviour that we expect from our leaders. Nevertheless, human nature has created a reality that even leaders need to take into account. In all aspects of society, we believe that we run more risk by doing something than by doing nothing. If you do something and it goes wrong, you will be punished: that is the basis of this reasoning. Your reputation will be damaged, your self-esteem will take a beating and you will need to wait for ages before you are given another chance to put things right. These are all elements that involve loss. And loss – cost, paying the price, call it what you will – is something that we want to avoid. In other words, people are more strongly motivated by a desire to prevent loss than they are by a desire to make gains.

The psychology of the leader

Viewed in these terms, it is not difficult to understand why leaders are often reluctant to take risks.[51] 'Not failing' is more important than 'succeeding'. Preservation is more important than change. And so nothing happens.

This is the irony of the current financial and economic situation, in fact, of all crisis situations. A crisis shows us in a rational manner that there are reasons to change, whereas our irrational human nature tells us that that there are reasons for doing nothing. Trapped in this dilemma, we tend to do the thing that comes most naturally to us, no matter how irrational it might seem. This tendency to do nothing in preference to doing something is referred to in the literature as the' omission bias', and is closely related to the 'status quo bias'.[52] Even when there are rational reasons to support a process of change – for example, the existence of reliable future predictions – people will still find it hard to break free from the emotional chains of the existing situation. Delay, inactivity, maintaining the status quo – these continue to 'feel' the most comfortable options. Particularly in difficult circumstances, where the taking of decisions requires even more energy than normal, our leaders often have the idea that 'If I don't do anything, I can't do anything wrong'. This attitude explains why in general we are more ready to forgive bad results arising from negative inaction than we are to forgive bad results arising from positive action. Indeed, research has proven that most people have a stronger and more positive conviction that you are 'less guilty' if you have done nothing, than if you have done something and got it wrong. This was nicely illustrated in an experiment in which the test subjects were asked to imagine that they were a judge awarding damages to a person who had suffered loss. For the first test group, the loss in question was caused by actions that someone had consciously taken. For the second test group, the loss resulted from the fact that someone had failed to take action. The damages awarded by the first test group were significantly higher. Enough said.[53]

To conclude, keep in mind the following:

(i) Change is not only a key element of leadership, but it can actually be very useful to develop future strategies and approaches. Specifically, by deciding to leave the status quo you obtain immediate feedback which enhances your learning skills and potential. Moreover, changing situations will add to your transforming qualities as a leader – a leadership style that has been demonstrated to be very effective in crises situations.

(ii) You don't let fear do the talking. Fearful decision-makers stick to what they have and thereby miss out on future opportunities to grow.

(iii) You do not search for too many alternative choices. It will not help you, rather it will paralyse you from actually making a decision.

(iv) Not doing anything in times of crisis may be safe at the personal level but is often damaging at the collective level.

Examples of leaders and the preference for the status quo

Jeffrey Preston 'Jeff' Bezos

In his job as founder and CEO of Amazon – an online merchant of books and related products – he is known to be a leader who challenges the status quo by means of his people-management style. Bezos is very keen on his employees being inventive and willing to experiment. He is a big fan of thinking out of the box and constantly checking whether improvements are possible – preferably in ways that haven't been tested before. Due to this encouraging and innovative style he manages to create a business climate in which the status quo is simply not accepted. His focus on 'doing better and preferably in different ways than before' earned him the Time Magazine's Person of the Year 1999 and a 2008 selection by the US News & World Report as one of the best leaders in the US.[54,55]

Xi Jinping

He is the current leader of the People's Republic of China. He is a leader who has expressed clear views on corruption, and political and economy reforms. He is described as being very much in touch with himself (authentic) and able to control his emotions, making the point that he can take thoughtful decisions. His decision-making is believed to be pragmatic, which will be useful to undertake his biggest challenge, which is to maintain the current economic reforms and state-based controls in relationship to a dynamic and international business scene that China will have to capitalise on. This challenge therefore includes an important leadership dilemma in which he has to try to strike a balance between reforms and adopting a status quo position.[56]

What are the alternatives?

Thus far, we have labelled procrastination – the postponement or avoidance of necessary decisions – as a form of irrational behaviour. A whole variety of emotions and distorted ways of thinking conspire together to ensure that our leaders act indecisively (if they act at all), throwing them into a negative spiral from which it is often difficult to escape. Of course, there are also numerous situations where it is possible for a leader to make a rational analysis, in which each choice is carefully weighed and measured. But does this make it any easier for that leader to take timely and effective decisions? Unfortunately, it does not. Here, too, there are a number of problems.

Viewed in rational terms, the making of a decision is easiest when there is clearly a superior option. In these circumstances, there should be no need for any further analysis before the right choice is made. As we have seen, however, our emotions sometimes get in the way of this simple logic. For example, inaction inertia may prevent us from making a decision. But even when our emotions are not involved, it is still not necessarily a simple matter to decide which choice is the 'best' choice. Sometimes there is very little difference between the various alternatives, and this certainly complicates the decision-making process. In other words, comparable alternatives can also be a reason for not taking positive action.

It is precisely for this reason that psychologist Bernard Nijstad argues that a careful evaluation of the differentiating features of the alternatives is a crucial first step for any decision-maker.[57,58] Can the alternatives can be differentiated on a number of different dimensions that are important to you in relation to the decision you need to make? Is this level of differentiation always important to you? Research has shown that the more important people regard the decision they need to make, the more difficult it becomes if the level of differentiation between the alternatives is small. And the reverse is also true: if a decision is perceived as being less important, the role played by the level of differentiation between the alternatives is also correspondingly less important.

Of course, it is perfectly possible that the level of differentiation between the alternatives is low because they are all equally good choices. Yet again, this does not make the final choice any easier, but it does mean that a decision will usually be taken. All the alternatives are deemed to be appropriate to the solving of your particular problem, so to some extent it doesn't really matter which one you pick. But it is a very different matter when the level of differentiation is small and all the alternatives are unattractive. Being forced to make a choice from a series of options that are all as bad as each other is a powerful motive for doing nothing. And so in these circumstances a decision will usually not be taken.

What should you do when you find yourself in this latter situation? The first obvious step is to investigate whether or not there are any other alternatives that are more attractive (or, at least, less unattractive). This implies, however, that you will need to look at the decision you need to make in a totally new light. In other words, you will need to think 'out

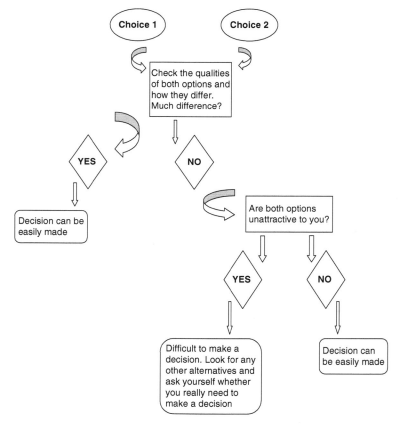

Figure 3 How to make choices between different alternatives

of the box' (as the jargon puts it). Your previous approach was clearly unsatisfactory, since it only resulted in alternatives that were universally unattractive. The situation therefore needs to be reinterpreted. Naturally, it is possible that you might not be able to come up with any better alternatives. If they exist, you probably would have considered them already. Then again, maybe not. It is certainly worth taking the time to check and make sure. If you find no new alternatives, or if the new alternatives are just as unattractive as the original ones, you may need to ask yourself whether or not it is really necessary or in your best interests to make a decision. Why are you moving in this direction if all your choices are bad ones? Is it really worth the effort? What can possibly be the benefits? These are important questions that you should not be afraid to ask yourself. Failing to take a decision can often be damaging, but so too can making a decision in a situation where you have nothing to gain – and perhaps everything to lose (see Figure 3 for a summary of the decision-making model).

Example of leadership being open to alternatives

François Hollande

He is the 24th President of the French Republic and defeated Nicolas Sarkozy in the race for the presidency. He is a socialist but has an eye for the wide range of alternatives available before taking a decision. He is credited for his fast thinking. According to his economic policy advisor Philippe Aghion, he is someone who understands a problem quickly and is able to swiftly assess costs and benefits. However, he does take this time to make a decision based on the available information and alternatives present. In fact, despite his thorough and quick mode of thinking he is extremely cautious in committing to a decision or action. As long as he remains equally pragmatic – as he has shown in the presidential elections – his open attitude to existing alternatives should reveal good decision-making. If the pragmatic attitude will be replaced by stronger party-based ideologies it can be expected that decisions will be delayed and reveal poorer outcomes.

Neuroticism

Leaders are not only capable of hampering the functioning of others, but also of themselves. The more society expects certain things, the more compelled leaders feel to keep things under their own close control. Young leaders in particular are inclined to play this power game, so that they often end up losing themselves in a mass of detail. This, too, can mean long delays before a decision is finally taken. Naturally, there is nothing per se wrong with the fact that a leader wishes to avoid making overhasty decisions. It does, however, become a problem when this pattern repeats itself time after time, without there being any real reason to justify such neurotic behaviour. It has been especially noticeable in recent years how many politicians have succumbed to this temptation to over-focus on details. The search for details can sometimes be necessary, but only if it has a positive effect on the final outcome of the decision-making process. All too often, it is simply a lack of resolution and the will to succeed, disguised as 'thorough preparation' – which has become yet another political euphemism for doing nothing. In this sense, discussion of details in political negotiations is being used increasingly as a tool for deferring a decision on the subject under discussion to some unspecified future date, in the hope that the problem might somehow go away or at least be reopened in conditions that are more favourable to your own position and interests.

A continual emphasis on detail when it is clearly not necessary usually betrays a strong fear of making an evaluation on the part of the decision-maker. This type of fear can result from an overly harsh self-evaluation, but also from a need to assess different interests that are difficult to reconcile. If the postponement of a decision is caused by an exaggerated fear of making a mistake, or by a desire to avoid making a poor evaluation, or by a compulsive need to exchange uncertainty for maximum security, it is possible (and perfectly reasonable) to describe the decision-maker as having a neurotic personality. Research has shown that neuroticism shares a negative correlation with effective leadership and that people with high levels of neuroticism also display high levels of decision avoidance and procrastination.[59,60,61]

The phenomenon of a neurotic tendency as a basis for procrastinating behaviour is evident in a number of different leadership styles. A neurotic leadership style is characterised by a certain way of thinking, a certain manner of regulating the emotions and a certain way of interpreting the facts. These characteristics express themselves through both the general functioning and the specific behaviour of the leader in question. One of the most noticeable features of each of these leadership styles is the fact that the leader is not someone who can easily absorb and assimilate new information in a manner which leads to a change in their way of thinking and acting. On the contrary, they show little interest in self-analysis and make little effort to assess the influence of certain situations and/or relationships correctly.

Several types of such neurotic leadership exist.

The 'high expectations' leader: Being too perfect for your own good!

This type of leader regards himself/herself as someone who knows what to do in all circumstances and has the necessary qualities to succeed. Leaders in this category think that they are always in the picture about everything, are analytical in their approach and are ultra-professional in their actions. Driven by their strong desire to achieve perfection and tackle problems 'root and branch', they tend to dominate the other people in their environment. This means, amongst other things, that they like to do everything themselves and have problems to delegate tasks and authority to others. In their eyes, these others are never competent enough to do what they can do. Being focused so much on their own excellent qualities makes them quick to criticise others when their own high standards and expectations are not met – as is frequently the case in their eyes. It therefore is no surprise that this leader type is quickly seen by people as arrogant and overconfident, which – for obvious reasons – will have a negative effect on the atmosphere in the work environment. Unfortunately, little can be done to improve the working climate as this leader seldom notices this negative tension, since he/she views everything exclusively from his/her own competitive frame of reference. Evaluating himself/herself and evaluating others is the only thing that counts.

High-expectations leaders are:

- Self-focused
- Analytical
- Ultra-professional
- Perfectionist
- Criticise others
- Do not delegate tasks
- Evoke negative impressions with others.

The 'furious' leader: When things don't go the way I like it!

Leaders with much fury employ an emotional decision-making style that is usually driven by feelings of frustration. For the majority of the time they appear to be normal, well-balanced individuals, but when they sense that their freedom is being restricted, they can explode with volcanic fury. These leaders express their emotions openly and directly to the outside world. They hold nothing back. Because they lack the capability to inhibit their emotions, they have difficulty in keeping things under control, which makes them jump from one thing to the next in an uncoordinated manner. Not surprisingly, these leaders fail to solve problems in an effective way, basing their strategic approach on a straight and immediate assessment of perceived advantages and disadvantages. The problems that they encounter as a leader are quickly experienced as personal problems, to which they then become very emotionally committed. In addition to this extrovert type of leader, there is also a more introvert type. They experience the same negative emotions as their counterparts, but are less inclined to openly communicate this to the outside world. They do possess some sense of control which makes them able to keep their feelings to themselves. In a way we could say that they are not active but rather passive in their aggression. Being passive in aggression does mean that these leaders are able to maintain a desire for 'getting back' at you over a long period, which makes them take rapid and unexpected action against the things and people that have irritated them.

Furious leaders:

- Can explode in fury
- Communicate their emotions openly
- Use short-term thinking and solutions
- Take everything personal.

The 'I love myself' leader: Being too narcissistic to lead others!

Some leaders are in love with their own personalities and develop a series of strategic measures to ensure that other people accept them, so that they can set about securing their own interests undisturbed. These narcissistic leaders only have one purpose: to let everyone else see just how fantastic they really are. They have such a strong desire to ensure that their superiority is universally recognised and unchallenged.

To achieve this objective, they can be charming, but at all times they are capable to stay rational enough to manipulate those whom they charm, so that these people can be used for the leader's purposes, when the need arises. As a result of this duality, no one can really say that they 'know' the person behind the leader. He/she remains very much an unknown quantity, yet this exact element of mystery adds further to his/her charisma. Having said this, once it becomes apparent that the leader is only concerned with his/her own interests, this charisma will obviously soon disappear. In a way, narcissistic leaders are confronted with two opposing motives that – ironically speaking – fuel their desire to put themselves in the middle of the attention. On one hand they are usually people with a strong 'winner's' mentality, while on the other hand they are fearful that others will sooner or later regard them as a failure. It is this attempt to achieve the perfect image which leads them to not being really interested in the general good of the group. They almost seem programmed to see 'life' as something in which they play the central role.

The 'I love' myself leader:

- Wants to show how great he/she is
- Is charming
- Has a strategic personality
- Is charismatic and mysterious
- Does not invest in the collective well-being.

The 'unpredictable' leader: When your impulses make decisions!

The decisions and actions of such leader types can be unpredictable to the extreme. You never know what they are going to do next. In fact, they often don't even know themselves. This is a result of their almost total lack of self-control. They do not believe in long meetings, where everything is discussed thoroughly. Instead, they prefer to exercise their own freedom of choice and action, making decisions when they feel the need – and not before. It is very difficult to reconcile the impulses of this type of leader with the rigidities of a formal structure in which the important strategic objectives of the organisation are framed. This lack of stability and direction makes many other people feel powerless, so that relationships do not run smoothly. In other words, impulsive leaders have a dysfunctional effect on their organisations, making it difficult to build up confidence and trust. Being so concerned with their own impulses creates an excessive focus on their own person, highlighting that with all their positive and negative qualities, they have little feeling for the general good of their environment. As a result, they pay almost no attention to the 'big picture', so that important strategic decisions often remain untaken or are hindered by their self-opinionated attitude. Their strong focus on their own person is fed by their desire to present themselves in the best possible light, which suggests that they have a strong fear of self-evaluation – as most neurotic personalities do. When trying to manage these leaders it is therefore important to allow them to develop a good feeling about themselves, while pointing out – and making them accept – that the organisation also needs authentic people who are prepared to run the risk to fail every now and then.

The unpredictable leader:

- Does not participate in long meetings
- Prefers situations where there is no control and looks for complete freedom
- Searches for personal power
- Is impulsive
- Does not pay attention to the big picture
- Has difficulties building trust

Example of neurotic elements in leadership

Nicolas Sarkozy

He served as the 23rd President of the French Republic from 16 May 2007 until 15 May 2012. His leadership style was characterised by being hyperactive and impulsive. His somewhat neurotic leadership style was reflected extremely well in the way he took care of his public image. He was, for example, named in the list of both best-dressed as worst-dressed persons in the world.

Best dressed by Vanity Fair, worst dressed by GQ[62,63]

> He also had a strong tendency to talk about topics and themes outside of his immediate expertise and was impulsive in communicating his beliefs on a wide variety of societal issues. For example, a few weeks before the start of 2007 presidential elections he argued that one is born a paedophile and that it is a disease that needs to be cured – although we do not know how yet. These kinds of statements were often criticised by scientists and journalists.[64]

The avoidance of conflict

Every decision you take has consequences for other people. Not everyone will be happy or in agreement with these consequences. Some people will think that the decision does not serve their best interests. Others will think that the decision does not conform to previously made agreements. Their expectations will not have been met, so that your relationship of trust comes under pressure. Whatever your motivation in taking the decision, there is a risk that its outcome may result in conflict of one kind or another.

Conflicts do not always have to be negative. Recent literature has shown that conflicts provide the necessary fuel and innovation for the growth of teams, groups and organisations.[65] In other words, conflicts can give people the opportunity to identify shortcomings and acquire new insights. Of course, it is important that the conflicts are managed in the right manner, if positive results of this kind are to be achieved. If this is not the case, the conflicts can indeed sometimes lead to escalation and the damage of mutual relations, so that the long term outcome is negative rather than positive. Moreover, different people will have different visions about the value of conflict for themselves and their environment. And it is indisputable that the concept of conflict still has many negative associations. This means that lots of people have developed a fear of being involved in conflicts. Consequently, they will do everything they can to avoid them. One of the most regrettable aspects of this conflict avoidance is that it may lead to the postponement or even the abandonment of decisions. If no decision is taken, its outcome cannot ignite or fuel a conflict situation.

This fear of conflict can also cause leaders to postpone their decisions. For this reason, it is important to create a context in which fear of conflict can be limited. What characteristics must this context display? First and foremost, it must be a context in which the different parties have experience of giving and receiving feedback. This openness can help to reduce the fear of conflict and allow differences in opinion to be seen as something constructive. As a leader, you can contribute to this process by using decision-making procedures that are regarded as honest and transparent by those around you. And the more honest your procedures appear, the greater the chance that your choices will be accepted. Studies have shown that the use of honest procedures (encouraging consultation, giving accurate information, allowing for retrospective correction, etc.) are seen by others as respectful. Transparency can therefore ensure that your relations with others remain intact and that the work culture is open and constructive.

The anticipation of conflict can be influenced by individual differences. For example, people with an intuitive way of thinking, who use their emotions as an important guide to their behaviour, will more quickly develop the expectation that others will not agree with them. For this reason, these individuals will also be more easily inclined to postpone decisions, since decisions are a possible source of the conflicts they anticipate. It is important for this type of leader that sufficient consultation is conducted before a decision is taken. A constructive opening phase is necessary to remove the fears and uncertainties. The greater the amount of information available about possible differences of opinion, the easier it becomes to assess the likelihood of possible conflict.

People can also differ in the extent to which they underestimate or overestimate the impact of their actions on their relationships. People who are highly sensitive and who always try to look at things from the other person's point of view will be quick to adjust their strategy to avoid a negative reaction from the other party. However, leadership also means that from time to time you must also take decisions on unpopular matters. The responsibilities of a leader include the breaking of bad news, which will often damage the interests of one or more of the parties involved. For this reason, it is important that all leaders should develop their own clear and realistic image of what leadership involves and should decide how they can strike a fair balance between task orientation and people orientation – a balance that must ensure that the fear of causing damage to the needs and expectations of others does not have a dominant influence on their decision-making process.

> ### Example of leadership not being afraid of conflicts
>
> #### Benjamin Netanyahu
>
> He is the current Prime Minister of Israel and widely known for his determined, courageous and decisive leadership style. His career is an example of excellent achievements in the military, political and economic realm. He has been referred to as a leader who is not afraid to voice his opinion, regardless of whether conflicts may be at stake or not. His efforts to make the world aware that the possible nuclear threat that Iran poses to Israel, the US and the whole region have made him a valued and strong leader on the global political scene. In his efforts he was, for example, not afraid to express a different opinion than Iranian President Mahmoud Ahmadinejad at the UN General Assembly in 2009.
>
> He is also regarded as highly authentic and able to make decisions in a timely and coherent way. Being the first Israeli Prime Minister who is actually born in Israel makes him very representative of the state and his leadership role in the military makes him credible in representing the Israeli. In those efforts, he has shown to be a leader who challenges the status quo and is able to make decisions under enormous pressure. These leadership skills led the Israeli to vote him the 18th-greatest Israeli of all time and the British magazine New Statesman to list him 11th on the list on the world's most influential figures in 2010.

Not being authentic

As has already been mentioned, decisions are not taken in a social vacuum. Every decision raises new issues that send the leader and his group along a new and different path. For this reason, one of the most important tasks for any leader is to make an assessment of the likely consequences of his/her decisions. It is even more important that the leader should be prepared to stand behind these consequences, although it is always necessary to first ensure that they are compatible with the values that he/she wishes to pursue and communicate, both as a leader and as a person. Many leaders find it difficult to adopt a clear position with regard to the consequences of their decisions. They beat about the bush and are not open about what will happen, why it will happen and how important it is. Perhaps not surprisingly, this makes them more inclined to postpone the decisions that bring them into this uncomfortable position: if there is no decision, there can be no consequences for which they will be held responsible (see also the concept of omission bias). In this way, it becomes unnecessary to use their own values to evaluate the decision–consequences correlation.

This is an important point, since many leaders do not have a high level of awareness of their own values. Or perhaps it is more correct to say that leaders do not stand sufficiently behind their own values. This typical situation has led to growing calls in recent years for a more authentic style of leadership. In fact, the literature on this subject has become compulsory reading for all modern, forward-looking leaders.[66] As a result, the concept of authenticity in leadership has developed from what was once a subsidiary characteristic into a major priority. Of course, it is one thing to read about being authentic and another thing to actually become so. And it is indeed open to question whether or not you can actually 'learn' to become authentic. Be that as it may, there are two key themes relating to authenticity in leadership that are important for helping to understand procrastinating behaviour.

Authentic leaders are assumed to be aware of their own strengths and weaknesses. These leaders are in contact with their feelings and needs. This means that they also have a better understanding than other leaders of the values that really motivate them. This high level of self-knowledge is a fruitful medium which encourages leaders to grow in their efforts to improve and transform the common good. But a high level of self-awareness does not mean that such leaders do not question themselves, their motives and their behaviour. On the contrary, being aware of your own values implies that as leader you must always ask yourself critical questions about the decisions you are required to make.

Their authenticity should ensure that these leaders are able to withstand external pressure and are able to remain 'true' to themselves, even when called upon to make difficult decisions. It is precisely this that neurotic leaders are *not* able to do. They find it impossible to critically examine their actions and refuse to face up to the consequences of their decisions. The advantage of being able to look critically at the things you do is that leaders of this type can work out for themselves why they might be inclined to postpone a decision. The leaders who are capable of this kind of self-assessment have the ability to search actively for solutions that can lower the threshold for decision-making. This means that over time authentic leaders gradually evolve a more decisive, less procrastinating style of leadership. They appreciate their own strengths and weaknesses, which allows them to make more balanced decisions, with which they feel comfortable. In most cases, they can avoid the negative emotions referred to in this chapter.

The concept of an authentic leader is an ideal that we should strive to achieve – but it is not always easy. As mentioned in the Introduction (Chapter 1) to this book, people are not perfectly rational, which means (among other things) that we are often blind to the things that can threaten our self-image.[67] As a result, we have a natural human tendency to ignore – both consciously and unconsciously – our weaknesses and failings. The need to protect our ideal image of ourselves, which is something we associate with our strengths, persuades us to sweep our shortcoming under the carpet. Out of sight, out of mind. This makes it difficult to 'learn' the art of authentic leadership. It takes years of experience and training to remain true to your ideals, when placed under the pressure that decision-making often involves. For this reason, it is advisable for all leaders to force themselves to confront their weaknesses and learn to deal with their insecurities.[68]

This is important, since every decision inevitably involves a degree of insecurity and uncertainty. There is always an internal contradiction in decision-making, which involves both gain and loss. There is gain, because a decision is made and the status quo is changed, hopefully for the better. But there is also loss, because the taking of a decision means that the door is now closed on other options, which you can no longer use. This internal contradiction encourages doubt, doubt that can be most easily overcome when you feel good about yourself and know exactly why you are taking a particular decision. And this is only possible if you have good self-knowledge, if you are fully aware of your own boundaries and limitations. In other words, understanding your own weaknesses makes you a better and a stronger decision-maker.

So, what are exactly the reasons why authentic leadership buffers against procrastination? As an authentic leader you:

(i) Are in contact with your own feelings and needs
(ii) Understand which values motivate you

(iii) Allow to question yourself in ways that does not motivate you to run away from the consequences of your actions
(iv) Allow yourself to manage uncertainty in positive rather than negative ways.

Of course, being authentic is much easier said than done. Why is it so difficult to achieve authenticity? It is important to know these elements as they can help to identify the challenges you need to work on as a leader. So, the traps preventing leader authenticity are as follows:

- The hardest thing is to know yourself. Although we have to live with ourselves for the rest of our lives, often we do not know ourselves very well. Due to our motivation to self-enhance and perceive ourselves in a positive light we particularly miss out on feedback concerning our failures and blindspots.

- Too much reliance on what others say you have to do. Humans are social beings and one aspect of a social identity is that we like to conform to the norms, attitudes and opinions of others. To survive in our society we, of course, need to be able to conform to some extent, but too many leaders become worried about their public image and forget completely about who they are and what they want to stand for.

- People find it too difficult to achieve valued ideals. Having a conviction is great, acting on it is even better. But it is the latter part that many leaders fail to develop. Acting on your ideals is considered by many an exhausting task, particularly since the achievements of ideals asks for hard work and dedication. For many among us this hard labour is something they are simply not willing to do.

- Lack of experience in making deals and business as a leader. It is necessary to understand that leader authenticity is not something that you can achieve at any moment in your leadership career. As with many things in life, achieving success takes time and developing a sense of authenticity is also something that is fed by experience. Being the new kid on the block as a leader is not a situation that asks immediately for an authentic contribution on your behalf. In fact, for those new leaders it is more important to learn and steal with your eyes to say so, to understand the leadership role – put it in context – and once you know what it is about start adding your personal touch to it.

Examples of leader's authenticity

Ronald Paul

He is a Republican politician who has been a candidate for President of the US three times. Despite his age, he turned out to be very popular among young voters in the 2012 Presidential campaign, making that the press referred to him as 'Mr. authentic'. Ron Paul has proven throughout his tenure in Congress that he has a clear vision and a stable set of values which he sticks to (e.g. he will never raise taxes and will not approve budget deficits). Because of his calm and authentic way of debating he comes across as sincere and as very much independent of the Republican's party rules (i.e. he collaborates with politicians across the party boundaries).

David Cameron

He is the Prime Minister of the UK. At age 43 he became the youngest Prime Minister of the last 198 years, setting high expectations for him to bring change to the fore. Unfortunately, Cameron has emerged as a politician regarded as not being very authentic. He often makes statements that he later on has to retract or put in perspective. His leadership style is criticised because he tends to pay too much attention to his image and adopts his behaviours and decisions too quickly to what people may think. For this reason, he is sometimes referred to as 'Dave the Chameleon' – a habit that he shares with this other famous chameleon Mitt Romney. Both politicians strive to match their actions to the expectations of the audience that they are facing.

Mamata Banerjee

She is the current and first female Chief Minister of West Bengal. Her victory was historic as it ended about 35 years of sclerotic communist ruling. What makes her very authentic is the fact that she steadily climbed up the ranks as an independent politician with her own views and mind. She is known to be very decisive – and sometimes even a little bit autocratic – because she knows what she stands for and has a clear vision for the country. She is seen as sincere and not driven by a need for power because she has maintained an austere lifestyle and endorsed the central role of family throughout her career. As many authentic leaders, she is able to emotionally appeal to her audience, making that she can touch the imagination and dreams of those willing to follow her.

CHAPTER 3
The psychology of the situation

It is also important for leaders to keep a cool head in moments of crisis, so that they can continue to analyse the situation in a rational manner that will lead to the best possible decision in the circumstances. Yet in spite of the existence of this ideal image on which to base their actions, it is remarkable to see how many leaders still find it difficult to make decisions. Procrastination seems to be the rule, rather than the exception. To some extent, this is a consequence of the personal characteristics and the personal way of thinking of the individual leader (see Chapter 2). The nature of the situation also has a strong effect on how the leader reaches a decision. Moreover, the leader is more than just a single individual. He/she is part of a group and is therefore subject to a wide range of social influences. It is surprising how many people continue to underestimate the impact of social factors on the thinking and actions of others, including leaders. Instead, there is a kind of automatic assumption that these thoughts and actions are largely determined by the personal preferences of the person concerned. Little or no account is taken of the social context and the force of the prevailing circumstances. We continue to focus stubbornly on the personality of the other person as the driving force behind their behaviour.[69]

In reality, however, our behaviour is strongly influenced – both implicitly and explicitly – by the situation in which we find ourselves. This means that our decisions – and our willingness to take them (or not) – are also influenced by situational factors. Each of these decisions – as we have already mentioned – has important consequences, not only for the leader, but also for others. This fact alone – that others are affected by the manner in which a leader makes a decision – means that the influence of the social situation should not be underestimated. In order to deal with the pressures inherent in this social situation, it is first necessary to understand which social influences are relevant to the decision-making process. This requirement is critical to the development of effective leadership leading to firm and clear decision-making. In fact, by increasing your understanding of the social context it will allow you to more easily make sense of the actions that you will have to take. In a way, understanding the social influences present helps you to determine which actions are more appropriate and will thus facilitate decision-making rather than hamper it. It is indeed true that an abundance of evidence exists showing that the social setting in which one moves around is a strong determinant of your behaviour, perceptions and motivations and ultimately how you feel about what you do. For this reason, it is important that as a leader you learn to look at social situations in a focused way that enables you to:

- Increase your situational awareness.
- Analyse specific features of the situation and how they relate to the decision that you have to make. In this respect, it is important to recognise what exactly is happening around you and how and in what way this may relate to the decisions that you will take and the consequences that will emerge from it.
- Analyse how situations – over time – differ in the demands that they pose and how these differences may shape your decisions.
- Identify the stakeholders that are involved in your decision. Put differently, based on the situation at hand you may more quickly get a grasp of who has a stake in the outcome of the decision and who has not. It is exactly this type of information you need to know when deciding about your strategy.
- Be clearer about the kind of relationships you will be able to develop and how these social connections can help or hinder efficient decision-making.

In this chapter we will identify several social factors and examine their impact, in particular with reference to the procrastinating behaviour of leaders.

Limited anonymity

Leaders are more in the spotlight than the rest of us. Because of their position of authority, they are constantly in the picture. Whether they like it or not, their actions are closely watched and widely reported. Almost every decision carries an element of responsibility for the leader. This means that they not only have to cut through often knotty problems but also have to weigh up the relative interests of the parties likely to be affected. In other words, they have to deal with opposing, sometimes irreconcilable differences and needs – and then justify the reasons for their choices. Being a leader is therefore a high-pressure job, since they cannot rely on the comforting shield of anonymity. But what exactly are the influences to which they are exposed as a result of this limited anonymity?

The lack of anonymity when taking a decision puts most leaders fairly and squarely in the firing-line. The public will assess the merits of the decision and the behaviour of the leader in terms that are highly diagnostic for the leader's personality. For those affected by the decision, the leader's personality will be coloured by what he/she does – or does not do. This level of social pressure means that leaders need to consider their decisions very carefully. Whatever they finally decide, they know in advance that it will inevitably help to shape their social image.[70] If your decision is perceived as 'good', others will be ready to praise you and follow your lead. If your decision is perceived as 'bad', you will be heavily criticised – and perhaps even worse. For each of us, our public image is an important part of the way in which we experience our own being. People have an important need for a strong sense of identity, and the nature of this identity is determined to a large extent by the social feedback we receive. Who we are reflects how we are evaluated socially by those around us. If there is no possibility to remain anonymous, there is every chance that the leader will regard the effects of the decision on his/her own social identity as being every bit as important as the content of the decision itself.

This potential conflict of interests means that decisions are not always taken in the best possible manner. If the likely pressure of negative social evaluation becomes too great, many leaders will have a tendency to postpone the decision or defer it indefinitely. Poor decisions would suggest to the world that he/she is not competent – and a social image of incompetence makes it very difficult to continue functioning as an effective leader. An unfortunate consequence of this heavy burden of social evaluation is that leaders sometimes get the feeling that they *must* do certain things. If they reach this stage, their decisions are more likely to be motivated by social vanity than by a rational assessment of the merits of the situation. Because we all have a need to present ourselves in a favourable social light, it is not always possible to hold our vanity in check. For this reason, it is extremely important that

The psychology of the situation

leaders should be aware of this fact and remain true to the principle that decisions must be made on the basis of what they want to do (for the general good) and not on the basis of what others think they should do.

In order to decide what they want to do, it is important to be able to separate the consideration of the issues at stake from the social pressure surrounding those issues. In this respect, being authentic (see Chapter 2) is a major plus-point. This requires the leader to make analyses in a manner that allows sensitive social information to be utilised in a generally useful way. This means in turn that it is vital not to look at things from a purely 'black-or-white' perspective, where one position automatically excludes another. Instead, it is necessary to try and develop a more integrative method of thinking. Integrative thinkers try to see the valid points in all the different arguments, before attempting to merge these into a coherent whole.[71] This is by no means a simple matter, and to avoid the possibility that the end result becomes over-complex, it is essential to give leaders the necessary time and space to conduct their deliberations calmly, so that they can bring the exercise to a satisfactory conclusion. In other words, leaders must have sufficient discipline and self-control to take decisions in an effective manner, notwithstanding the great social stress that they will often be under.

One of the underlying problems of non-anonymous situations is that the attention of the leader is concentrated on his/her own self-image, which costs huge amounts of mental energy. This absence of anonymity causes a huge drain on the leader's mental resources, so that often there is little left in the tank to focus on the all-important integrative elements of the decision-making process. As a result, the leaders often feel that they are no longer in 'the right frame of mind' to take a decision, and so they postpone and delay. In the literature, the feeling that someone is not in a position to coordinate all the necessary tasks because of a lack of energy is known as 'ego-depletion'.[72] In much the same way that your muscles get tired because they are no longer able to generate new energy, so leaders under great social pressure can also find it impossible to replenish their energy resources, with a consequent reduction in the quality of their decisions as a result. For this reason, it is important that leaders should bear in mind a number of basic principles that can lead to a healthier and more energetic life (see Chapter 8 for more details on how to achieve this). Table 4 outlines the challenges that lack of anonymity brings along and what to do.

TABLE 4 Challenges when dealing with increased accountability as a decision-maker

Challenge 1: Lack of anonymity creates a conflict between maintaining and protecting your social image and your need to deliver a message with content and – sometimes – opposing views to what the public wants.

Steps to take:

- *Be authentic:* get to know yourself and try making a distinction between what is really important to you and what is important because others think it is important.
- *Promote your integrative thinking:* being narrow-minded is not going to help you as it will only add even more pressure. You have to be able to develop a comprehensive view on the problems you are facing as a leader and integrate all the viewpoints possible to develop (and execute!) a plan of action.

Challenge 2: The more accountable your decisions become the more you can feel drained when decisions are hard to make.

Steps to take:

- *Be passionate about what you do and say:* If you do not feel passionate about the direction people think you should choose as a leader, it is time to reflect on this decision and whether you really want to take it. If you feel no passion, don't do it! If you feel passion, go for it but do not forget to always know why you are doing what you are doing.
- *Guard your level of energy:* Being able to deal with social pressures over time requires that you can find energy within yourself. It is therefore important to adopt a healthy lifestyle and exercise sufficiently. Make sure you have a clear head that allows you to take the occasional – and much needed – breathe of air.

A climate of distrust

It will come as no surprise that the manner in which we relate to each other is largely determined by levels of mutual trust. If people trust each other, it is possible to speak of a constructive atmosphere, in which information is shared and positive expectations can develop.[73] In relationships characterised by a high degree of trust, people will not feel threatened by the possibility of exploitation. It is therefore with good reason that trust is often referred to as the *social glue* of relationships. The presence of trust helps people to 'click', allowing them to form lasting and meaningful associations. Of course, the reverse is also true. As soon as something goes wrong, for whatever reason, levels of trust begin to fall. The presence of trust therefore implies that it can be damaged or lost altogether. Situations with low levels of trust are not supportive and often counterproductive. People feel vulnerable and look at each other with suspicion. As a result, they are less open, since they fear that they will not be fairly treated by the other side.

The psychology of the situation

Unfortunately, it is precisely this spirit of uninhibited open-mindedness that is necessary if the relationship between leaders and followers is to run smoothly. By virtue of their exalted position and status, leaders are regarded by many of us as people who can exercise an influence on the things that are important to us. In this sense, they possess a degree of power to shape the future of their followers – both positively and negatively. It is therefore important for leaders that they be seen as trustworthy and reliable, so that they can win the support of others.[74] If leaders feel that they are supported, they will be more strongly motivated to defend the collective interests of the group. In other words, the existence of trust can help to stimulate the taking of the right decisions.

However, the opposite also applies. An absence of trust can have a negative impact on the decisions of leaders. This distrust can take many different forms. Perhaps it is the leader who does not trust the followers. In these circumstances, the leader will not be prepared to risk his/her own position for the sake of others, and so will be inclined to postpone decisions. Why should he/she take a chance? If the decision turns out to be the wrong one, there is little likelihood that the followers will respond constructively and with understanding. Probably quite the reverse. Viewed from this perspective, it is safer to do nothing.

It is also possible, of course, that the followers have no confidence in the leader. It is vitally important for a leader to know whether this is the case or not. If a leader knows that his/her followers have lost their faith in his/her abilities, the leader will once again be reluctant to take risks. If decisions are taken at all, they will only be taken slowly and with great care. In most cases, the decisions that are taken will be viewed with such suspicion by the followers that they will have no real effect. This will be doubly the case if the leader displays any lack of competence. The absence of competence and expertise is a natural determinant of procrastinating behaviour. If the leader has no confidence or no knowledge of the matter in hand, he/she will be much more likely to adopt a defensive posture and play the status quo card. Serious choices will be postponed indefinitely.

The situation is potentially even more disastrous if the leader is not aware that the group has lost confidence in his/her abilities. In these circumstances, the leader is blind to the realities of the situation and therefore risks taking decisions on the basis of incomplete or faulty information, since little or no feedback is forthcoming from the followers. This is a recipe for bad decisions, which can quickly lead to an escalation of frustration and mistrust between the leader and the followers. Not surprisingly, this makes the taking of new decisions in the future even more difficult – and therefore less likely.

A climate of distrust can therefore have a negative influence on the decision-making process. For this reason, it is important that every possible effort should be made by the leader to build up and maintain the trust of the followers. To achieve this, it is first necessary to know what kind of information people use when assessing whether or not someone is trustworthy and reliable (see Table 5). Research has shown that there

---

TABLE 5 The challenge of building trust

What to do for being perceived as trustworthy?

Dimensions that you need to influence:

- *Competence:* One of the first things people look at in leaders is whether they have the necessary abilities to do the job. These abilities are very much related to the specifics of your job. So, people will look for information that confirms your expertise.
- *Integrity:* Equally important to competence is that followers expect their leaders to have a sense of integrity. This may be motivated because they want to work for fair and honest leaders because they do not want to be cheated upon. Rather, people wish to be protected by their leaders when needed.
- *Benevolence:* If you can develop relationships with others based on clear expectations but at the same time give you the latitude to bring commitment in the relationship that is not only based on cognitive but also emotional binding, you are leading for the long term.

Behaviours that you need to show:

- *Behavioural consistency:* If you decide to show a certain leadership style it is best to stick to it and if you need to change some elements of it do it gradually. People consider consistent behaviour as an indicator of your reliability.
- *Behavioural integrity:* Act on your words. If you say one thing but do another, you will lose people's trust quickly.
- *Promoting participation:* If you want followers who feel competent and in control to do their job as best as possible they need to feel your trust. One way of doing this is to give people a sense of input. People feel satisfied and respected if they know that their opinion is listened to. In addition, it creates relationships that are considerate and based on mutual respect. Of course, this participative process does not imply that you have to satisfy everyone's wishes. It simply indicates that people are looking for – albeit symbolic – signals that they are part of the company or collective you are leading. It is clear that at the end of the day your job is about making decisions that integrate and not respond to everyone's personal needs.
- *Using clear and transparent communication:* Too often, followers feel uncertain and even unsafe in their relationships with authority because too much attention is focused on the outcome and not on the process that leads to that outcome. As a result, many people are unclear about what happened and how to change things in the future, making commitment go down over time.

are three dimensions that are particularly relevant in this respect.[75] The first dimension is *competence*. People need to know that their leader is competent and that he/she will display this competence when making decisions. He/she must be seen as an expert in the fields of activity for which he/she is responsible. In people's minds, competence is a flexible concept. In other words, they assume that skills and competencies can be learnt. This means that we are more inclined to give people a second chance if they have failed in a matter relating to competence. However, if leaders fail in the second key dimension – *integrity* – we are less likely to be forgiving. This is not a flexible concept. Once we have it in our minds that a person lacks integrity, the idea remains firmly rooted and cannot be shifted: once bad, always bad.[76] People will only have confidence in their leaders if they see that they are true to certain moral principles, principles that are reflected in their behaviour. Leaders must do what they say; they must 'walk the talk'. Inconsistent behaviour suggests doubtful integrity. The third key dimension is *benevolence*. A leader will be regarded as benevolent if he/she makes it clear that he/she is prepared to defend the interests of the followers. This means that followers expect leaders to make a positive contribution towards the build-up of constructive relationships within the organisation. The relational aspect of this dimension is seen as an important factor in the concept that trust can act as social lime, bring people closer and more firmly together. Leaders who are able to make a good impression in terms of these three dimensions will win higher levels of trust from their followers.

In addition to the three key dimensions, there are other actions that leaders can take to show that they are reliable representatives.[77] As already mentioned, it is vital that leaders display consistency. This means that they first need to be clear in their own minds about the course they have steered in the past and the course they want to steer in the future. They also need to be aware that there are two forms of consistency on which they will be judged by their followers. The first is 'behavioural consistency', which means that actions must be consistent across time and in different situations. The second is 'behavioural integrity', which means that promises must be honoured and followed up. If there are regular discrepancies between what you say and what you do, your credibility will melt like snow on a warm spring day. As a separate issue, it is also necessary for leaders to show that everybody counts. Followers like to have the feeling that they are able to contribute input to decisions that affect the general good; in other words, their own good. This sense of participation is important for two reasons. Firstly, the followers will experience a sense of control. By taking part in the decision-making process, they will be convinced that they have been able to exercise a degree of influence, however limited, on the final outcome. Secondly, the relationship between leader and followers will be strengthened, since the followers will feel that their opinions are valued and respected. Being shown respect by their leaders is a key determinant for followers in terms of feeling comfortable within the group or organisation.[78]

Finally, it is important that leaders should communicate correctly with their followers. Leaders who are able to explain in a clear and convincing manner why they have taken a particular decision will usually enjoy greater support. The provision of logical feedback is experienced very positively by followers. The extent to which things are explained sensibly and accurately allows people to give meaning to the decisions that have been taken, which makes it easier to accept those decisions. This is particularly true if the results of the decision are not positive: followers then need a series of reasons that will allow them to put the situation in a proper perspective.[79] In these circumstances, it is vital that the leader should employ a clear and transparent communication strategy, based on the most reliable information.

Examples of leaders working with trust and distrust

Wang Yang

He is the current Secretary of the Guangdong Committee of the Communist Party of China and regarded widely as someone able and willing to reform Chinese top leadership. He is pragmatic but also shows concern for the interest of those who he leads, trying to reform the Guangdong province towards greater economic and political freedoms and by paying attention to the individual's needs when he wanted to re-instate the May Day week long holiday. His actions taken after the Wukan protests in 2011 made him a reliable and trustworthy leader in the region. After the villagers of Wukan revolted against local authorities, Wang Yang approved new local elections for a new village chief and ordered an investigation into possible cases of corruption. Because of his more interpersonal leadership style, Wang is believed to bring a softer touch to the top leadership in China.

Barack Obama

He is the current and first African American President of the United States. Due to his international actions he has managed to build an image of being trustworthy and competent. He received praise for his promise to end the combat operations in Iraq. At the end of August 2010 he officially declared that the US mission in Iraq was over and in October he noted that all the troops would be home for the holidays, enabling him to work on family values and benevolence. Another great illustration of his ability to be decisive and as such to promote trust was his decision to send the Navy SEALs to go after Osama Bin Laden. Bin Laden was killed in the mission and important information and files were acquired. In his role as commander-in-chief he seemed stable and confident, making him a trustworthy leader in the eyes of many (even across party boundaries!).

Uncertainty

During our lives we are regularly confronted with situations that make us feel uncertain or insecure. A world in which we are able to control everything simply does not exist. Uncertainty is therefore an important part of our experience of life. The making of decisions is one of the many things associated with this feeling of uncertainty. Yet although it is a feeling that we are all familiar with, it is still something that we are anxious to avoid. Uncertainty is a condition that people experience aversively. In other words, people are highly motivated to eliminate this condition from their lives – at least, as far as possible. The feeling that we can exercise control over what we do and the results that we achieve are a more comforting one and increase our levels of self-confidence. This means that we have a strong belief in the idea that we must try to control the uncontrollable.[80] This is clearly not possible – but it doesn't stop us from trying. We are eager to experience the illusion of control. This attempt to achieve a 'false' feeling of control is therefore, in reality, irrational behaviour. And an aspect of this behaviour, which we often use in our attempt to trick ourselves in this manner, is the postponing of decisions.

Procrastination is irrational because it is really a form of self-sabotage. The postponing of decisions appears to give us a feeling of control. The taking of a decision always implies the surrender of a certain degree of control, in the sense that the decision becomes 'public' and will be followed by visible results of one kind or another. By postponing the decision or continuing to 're-evaluate our position', we believe that we are somehow retaining a higher degree of influence over the situation: this is the illusion of control. In reality, however, the postponing of decisions is simply a way of avoiding the real issues, which creates even greater uncertainty. For this reason, leaders who fail to make decisions are ultimately seen as being irresponsible. This perception leads to unsatisfactory relationships within the organisation. Trust suffers and conflicts surface more easily. Of course, these are all factors that can encourage even more procrastination (see the concepts of climate of distrust and the avoidance of conflict). At the same time, other work processes will be hampered, so performance diminishes. The postponing of decisions to avoid feelings of uncertainty therefore creates more uncertainty in the long run.

This is contradictory to the ideas for which leaders are supposed to stand. Leaders are expected to make clear to others where the organisation's priorities rest, which values must be promoted and what we can all do to help realise our common objectives. In other words, one of the important tasks of a leader is to reduce our feeling of uncertainty – not increase it.

Because leaders are not always able to postpone decisions and because procrastinating behaviour is strongly influenced by the situation, it is important that leaders have at their disposal a number of weapons that can help to diminish the feeling of uncertainty experienced by their followers.

In these circumstances, it is important as a leader that the following are ensured:

(i) The objectives of the organisation and the responsibilities of each follower are clearly communicated. This can be done either formally or informally.

(ii) The objectives and expectations are communicated both in a public and in a private manner. If, as leader, you want to create a climate in which the members of your organisation talk to each other about their performance, they first need to know where each other's responsibilities rest.

(iii) You must ensure that a consistent and transparent evaluation system operates within the organisation, which monitors the extent to which these responsibilities are being met. Ensure also that this system is accepted by everyone as being a fair and legitimate instrument.

The psychology of the situation

(iv) You must describe clearly the time frame within which objectives must be achieved. People need deadlines, because if left to their own devices they will usually underestimate the time necessary to do the job (see Chapter 2 and the concept of the planning fallacy).

(v) You must learn to cope with uncertainty. You can do this by first recognising that we all like to maintain the illusion of control. Illusions do not help you to perform better; instead, they create hidden dangers of which you must be aware. In other words, it is better to accept the uncertainty of the situation, however uncomfortable it might feel, rather than trying to run away from this uncertainty, by pretending that it does not exist. The realisation that uncertainty is something you need to accept will create space in which you can develop new ways of thinking and working. It can help you to look at things in a different light, so that you will be able to make use of other sources of information. This, in turn, will help you to better assess your actions and decisions. Remember, however, that it is important not to be too ambitious. The awareness that uncertainty is always present argues in favour of moving gradually towards your objectives, so that situations of possible escalation can be avoided.

Leaders and dealing with uncertainty

Sheryl Sandberg

She is the current chief operating officer of Facebook and was named in 2012 as one of the 100 most influential people by Time. Her leadership style is characterised by a high level of energy and passion. She loves what she does and she knows how to communicate it. Due to her relentless optimism to see opportunities in every challenge she is able to inspire those who do business with her. Her decision to focus on advertisements rather than only creating cool sites made Facebook profitable, enabling the company to deal with unforeseen challenges in the future in a better way. As such, uncertainties are to her simply obstacles that can be removed. She applies this kind of thinking and energy to help Facebook make a difference in the world on how to connect.

Hillary Rodham Clinton

She was the first Lady of the United States when Bill Clinton was president and was the 67th US Secretary of State, serving in the administration of

(Continued)

> President Barack Obama. In recent years she has demonstrated her abilities to deal with uncertainties in constructive and thoughtful ways. In uncertain and turbulent times she has been credited to have strengthened the relationships between the US and its allies and at the same time to have convinced other non-ally countries to join in facing challenges of global order, such as threats from Iran. By being patient, knowledgeable and a loyal team player she has convinced many countries of the values and leadership of the US today. Because she knows what she wants and can be tough-minded in pursuing her vision, she enjoys support and legitimacy to negotiate and discuss issues that at first sight seem impossible. As such, she is able to reduce uncertainties and go to work to reshape relationships. For example, during her annual talks with Chinese leaders she was able to create a solution for the fate of the blind legal activist Chen Guangcheng (he eventually was allowed to travel to the US to study there).

Making ethical decisions

The decisions made by leaders have consequences for a number of different parties. First of all, there are consequences for the interests of the leader himself/herself. There are also consequences for the interests of his/her followers. This perspective makes clear that leaders possess a form of social power. Social power therefore allows leaders to exert an influence on the future and the interests of many other people in both a positive and a negative manner. This means that every decision taken by a leader can be judged on the basis of moral principles. Making use of moral values as a method of evaluating decisions has become a tried and tested technique with both the media and an increasing number of followers in recent years.

We live in a time where values such as sustainability and long-term thinking are part and parcel of people's mental processes. We can no longer avoid these concepts (even if we should wish to do so). This means that the actions of leaders are placed under an ethical microscope every time they are required to make an important decision. Just how this microscope is focused depends to a certain extent on the people involved and also on the strength of the 'us' against 'them' feeling inherent in the situation (moral inclusion versus moral exclusion).[81] Morality is very much 'in the eye of the beholder', which implies that it can be influenced by the position people take relative to the leader. This heavy moral responsibility is something that can paralyse many leaders in certain circumstances.

In other words, the strong focus placed on ethical decision-making can, paradoxically, lead to wrong decisions – or even no decisions – being taken. This is paradoxical because in certain religions the essence of ethics and morality is punctuality. In fact, within many religions procrastination is seen as hindering ethics. For example, in the Christian Bible we can read that Jesus considered reconciling with our adversaries as something that should be done immediately (Matthew 5: 23–24). In reality, however, many contemporary leaders either delay decisions because they become uncertain when faced with the moral imperatives involved or else they take lightweight decisions that seek to avoid the moral imperatives altogether.

Does this mean that we should not try to place our leaders under moral pressure when they are making their decisions? No, it does not! It does, however, mean that it is not always possible for leaders to use absolute ethical principles to weigh up each of their decisions. Each different set of followers may have a different ethical point of view, so that absolute standards cannot easily be applied. To complicate matters further, people have a natural human tendency to evaluate the results achieved by a decision in a very rational manner, which means that at this point they do apply absolute ethical principles. Put simply, this means that we apply a subjective interpretation of ethics before a decision is taken and an absolute interpretation of ethics after the decision has been taken. Little wonder that leaders sometimes dither and delay! For example, this contradiction makes it very difficult to take generally acceptable political decisions. And the complications don't end there. It is frequently overlooked that the results under consideration are often the result of a process that was also far from rational. People are not 100% perfectly rational, and this applies equally to our moral compass: it is also subjectively coloured.

Consequently, we know in advance what each individual ethical principle involves, but we can never be certain that the results will follow perfectly in the line of our ethical expectations. This means that we need to adopt a more nuanced approach to the interpretation of decisions. Moreover, it must be an anticipatory approach that reduces the likelihood of procrastination and helps to ensure that progress can be booked. Progress is very much a trial-and-error process, where it is sometimes necessary to take one step backwards in order to move two forwards. This means that it is virtually impossible for a decision to perfectly reconcile all the conflicting interests at stake – so that it is equally impossible to comply with absolute moral standards. For this reason, we need to develop a new model, a way of looking at decisions that takes account of the irrationalities of human nature.

Supporters of this idea argue that this must lead to a fully open culture, in which each party can contribute input on the basis of an equal position. This will result in a more finely nuanced moral evaluation of the majority of decisions. This, in turn, will make it possible to correct certain consequences and steer the decision-making process in a different direction.[82] In this way, moral principles can be shaped by social forces, which will result in a more realistic ethical evaluation when leaders are called to account.

At the same time, it is also possible for this kind of open culture to lose its necessary balance, so that an impasse may result. This, for example, is a much-heard criticism with regard to the so-called Dutch polder model: a model where people can continue to talk and talk, so that few decisions ever get taken. This shows that it is important to achieve equilibrium between the different moral principles that are grounded in the existing social reality, but without going to excessive lengths to gather more and more new opinions.

Viewed from this perspective, some people argue that a well-organised dictatorship can sometimes be more effective than a badly organised democracy. Of course, it is taking things too far if we start singing the praises of dictatorship – this goes against the basic moral principles of freedom and equality that are built into our human DNA. Even so, it underlines the importance of striking the right balance of rights and responsibilities in any consultative model. It is certainly true that the pressure exerted by the moral principle of equality means that there is a strong desire to achieve social cohesion, and this can indeed lead to a slowing down of the decision-making process. This is not necessarily a problem, as long as it does not open the door to situations where ideologies gain the upper hand over constructive interactions based on the facts of the matter under consideration. All too frequently, discussions and decision-making processes have a tendency to become ideologically tinted, which encourages the formulation of decisions in terms of rules and regulations. This increasingly bureaucratic approach is usually focused on making clear to people the responsibilities they are expected to bear. In other words, more rules must make more people more aware of their rights and obligations. Or that, at least, is the theory. Unfortunately, it does not usually work in practice.

It certainly strengthens the idea of 'my rights' but not the idea of 'my responsibilities'. The more rules you have and the more complex they become, the less inclined people are to judge themselves consciously against their perceived obligations. A culture in which everything is arranged by rules and regulations will always clash with the idea of a culture in which active and decisive leaders arrange matters by making strong decisions. There must, of course, be input into the decision-making process, and this input may come from several sources. But at the end of the day, somebody – a leader – has to decide what to do (see Table 6 for some important reflections).

> ### *Example of leadership not taking immediate ethical actions*
>
> ### Scott Walker
>
> He is a Republican politician currently serving as the 45th Governor of Wisconsin who became nationally known when the Wisconsin budget repair bill was criticised for alleged favouritism and patronage. The bill would scrap collective bargaining rights for most public sector workers. Months of mass protest asking for a recall election was undertaken. Such an election took place on 5 June 2012, which Walker survived. Walker himself did not expect such extreme reactions, but admitted that these sensitive (fairness) issues should have been dealt with in a more capable way when he asserted that 'if there was any mistake I made throughout all of this, I probably should have spent more time talking about the problems and then immediately fixing them'.

TABLE 6 The challenges of ethical decision-making

Ethical challenges to procrastination

Challenge 1: *Ethics is in the eye of the beholder*

The meaning of ethics and deciding what is ethical and what is not is a very subjective process. Our human biases influence people's striving to maintain positive self-views, making unethical actions justified to some extent. Because of this biased perception, it becomes increasingly more difficult to adhere to existing norms and values, as the situation may provide us with different frames of reference. As a result, depending on the situation, our interpretations change and what is judged appropriate or not is changed accordingly. Because both the leader and his/her audience may not share the same interpretations it becomes difficult to make a decision that everyone will agree with.

TABLE 6 (Continued)

Challenge 2: *It is a good thing to ask other's opinions, but someone needs to make a decision*

As noted earlier, being accountable and having a large crowd to please may hinder decision-making. If one is morally accountable, making decisions may come to a stop completely. Because many leaders fear of being evaluated negatively in terms of integrity and morality, decisions are delayed by extending the time used to consult with everyone. Of course, giving voice to all parties involved is a fair and honest thing to do. It signals to people that they are respected and that their opinion matters. Unfortunately, it does not help efficient decision-making if the procedure to give voice is simply a strategy to make sure that how you are evaluated morally is delayed. As a leader, you will have to make a decision and in this process it is important that the group is aware that a decision has to be made and that a consensus exists on the kind of dimensions that will be used to evaluate the morality of your decision.

Challenge 3: *More rules do not make people more aware of their rights and obligations*

Many leaders and companies adopt the idea that people are rational beings and that for this reason they will know what to do if the good behaviour gets rewarded and the bad one punished. Unfortunately, as discussed earlier, people are not completely rational – their biases more often than not influence decision-making. Nevertheless, a solution preferred by many leaders is to implement rules dictating what is expected. The rational idea behind it is simple: if you know what to do there should not be a problem. Research, however, shows that adding more rules adds complexity to the decision-making process and this degree of complexity in fact reduces – rather than increases – moral awareness of followers. Put it more exactly, the more rules you use the less likely it will be that followers develop their own moral judgements. For this reason, it is necessary that leaders work actively with followers on constructing values that are collectively endorsed. The advantages are that it is clear what is expected, that values are endorsed by all and that action can be taken rather than inaction becoming a second nature.

The new leader

The prospect of being appointed to a position of leadership can be a strong motivating factor for employees. To such an extent, that achieving leadership sometimes becomes a kind of mission, to which they attach the highest expectations. An idea frequently held by leaders-to-be is that a leader's position will allow them to fulfil their ambitions in life (or some of them, at least). This romantic and all-too-human image of leadership leads us to underestimate the daily tasks and challenges facing our leaders.[83] Research has shown that people are consistently wide of the mark when asked to predict their future reactions. For example, people are generally happier dreaming about promotion than when promotion finally comes along.[84] Similar misconceptions can also lead us to underestimate the responsibilities of leadership and to misjudge how we are likely to react once those responsibilities are ours. And it is certainly indisputable that the transition from follower to leader has far-reaching consequences in a number of different domains. Dealing successfully with this transition period – and the unanticipated problems it often throws up – is essential for the future of your leadership career. For this reason, it is important to know which challenges a new leader is most likely to encounter (see Table 7 for a summary of those challenges).

The first challenge is a *social* one. Your new position as leader will give a different dynamic to your relations with others. Before you became a leader, you had roughly the same status and authority as every other follower. You were all more or less on the same level. But not anymore. Your new position will force them to look at you – and you to look at them – in a fundamentally different manner. Henceforth, a power dynamic is involved in your relationship. You now have much more authority and responsibility than they do, so that the difference in your respective status becomes magnified. Many new leaders experience considerable stress as a result of this change in their relations with others. They do not yet have their new responsibilities fully under

---

TABLE 7 The challenges of a new leader

Social challenges

- *Your status changes:* When being promoted to the leadership role, people will start looking at you differently. A new position also means a new status and it is important that you become aware of this as quickly as possible. This difference in status will have implications for every action and decision you will have to take as your interest and the interest of others will be different.

- *Working on relationships with those who used to be your peers:* Now you are the leader in the group you will quickly realise that although the people around you are the same as when you were not the leader they are in a way not the same anymore. They now have to listen to you. Yesterday you were equals and working for someone else, today you are not equals anymore because the others are now working for you. This requires a change in mindset but also a different attitude in your relationships with the others. Establishing new norms in terms of interactions will be an important task.

Challenges regarding your competence

- *You will be evaluated in a different way than before:* Being the leader also increases your accountability and will increase the likelihood that you will be evaluated more critically. Be aware that bosses are under scrutiny and will be criticised in both public and private ways.

- *Know what you want to achieve in your new role:* Because you will be criticised you do need to develop a plan of action that corresponds to your new role. Become aware of how your position is changed and what this change implies with respect to the tasks and responsibilities you will now have.

control, but they can no longer ask their former friends and colleagues for advice the way they used to. As a leader, you are expected to know these things for yourself. From now on, people will look to you to give a lead. You are supposed to provide answers – not ask questions! This new situation therefore involves your first serious challenge as a leader: how can you redefine and further develop your changed relationships with others?

Here are some of the things that you can do as a new leader to feed your relationships with others in a positive way:

- Lead with passion. Show that you are passionate about your new position and that you are motivated to accept the responsibilities it entails. This will demonstrate that you intend to be an important reference point for others. A passionate approach is often contagious and will improve the atmosphere in your work environment, while at the same time creating space to motivate others.

- Make good and clear agreements with your followers – and then stick to them. The balance in your relationship has changed, so that it is important to clearly map out and give shape to new expectations on both sides. As previously mentioned, it is vital that you then pursue a consistent policy in the light of these agreements. In this way, you also build up a certain kind of legitimacy that is based on something more than the fact that people like you – which was a more important factor when you all had the same status.

- Be a 'people's' manager. Communicate clearly your belief as leader that it is your people who will ultimately make the difference. This means that you emphasise the importance of developing positive relations for the fabric of the organisation and for the creation of an atmosphere of trust.

- Be present, and make your presence felt. As a new leader, you can sometimes have the tendency to avoid your former colleagues and shut yourself up in the details of your new job. This is a mistake. Your new followers must be aware of your presence in the new situation and must feel your influence on events and on their actions. They must experience a feeling of solidarity between you and the rest of the organisation. This does not mean that you need to be involved in everything that happens – you must never be afraid to delegate – but make clear that you are aware of the things that your people are concerned about.

The psychology of the situation

The second challenge is located at the level of *competence*. By accepting a position of leadership, you can be certain that others – the people who are now your followers – will look at your more critically. They will check to see whether or not you have the competences that justify you being given the leader's job. During this phase, you must be clear in your own mind (and make clear to others) exactly what it is you want to achieve and exactly how others can help you to realise these goals. With this aim in mind, you should try to develop a strategy with the following elements:

- Take action that allows you to make a good impression within the organisation in a relatively short period of time. In the beginning, this means that it is better to focus on quick and easy successes, even if they are relatively minor. The big successes can wait for later, once everyone is on your side. It is also necessary during this phase to develop a clear vision for the future. Being open about your final objective will be appreciated by your people, but the most important thing of all is to make sure that you do not lose their support along the way. And the best way to bind your followers to your cause is to show that you are worthy of their trust and confidence. In this respect, every little victory, no matter how small, can help to bring you a step closer to your final destination.

- Draw up a list that outlines your most important projects for both the short term and the long term. To strengthen support for your leadership during your first few months in your new role, it is crucial to ensure that the initial short-term projects are successful. At the same time, it is important to make a connection between these projects and your final objective, so that people never lose sight of this objective and understand that their current efforts, even though they may seem relatively minor, are also contributing towards ultimate success.

- Analyse the strengths and weaknesses of your people, so that you can put your best people in the right places. Each of your followers will have his/her own unique qualities. It is your task to ensure that these qualities are used to maximum advantage in your initial short-term projects and beyond.

- Stimulate people to think about your organisation. What does it stand for and in what direction should it travel? Reflecting on these matters will help to create a strong feeling of solidarity. It will also allow you to start a learning process, to which everyone is free to offer input. In this way, you will be able to lock in the talents of others to the strategy that you have developed to realise your long-term objectives.

Example of new leadership being decisive

Tim Cook

As the successor of Steve Jobs, he is currently the new CEO of Apple.
In terms of leadership, no more difficult challenge seems to exist than to succeed someone as legendary as Steve Jobs. It has to be someone special to fill his shoes. Until now, however, Tim Cook has exactly done that in his own unique leadership style. Cook has already introduced several innovative decisions and policy changes, making that his leadership is accepted and that Apple is managed in ways that facilitate design breakthroughs even further. He is known for his discipline and ethics but also for his ability to be tough-minded when decisions have to be made. In his view, becoming the new leader requires preparation and hard work if you want to execute well and take decisions in a successful manner.

The lack of previous success

A lack of previous success can weigh heavily on the decisions that a leader will be required to make in the future. In fact, the pressure exerted by the weight may be so great that the leader is inclined to postpone these future decisions, so that he/she does not fail again. This is an understandable reaction, but hardly an efficient one. The postponement of decisions in this manner simply serves to create ever greater uncertainty, which makes it even harder to achieve success in the future. People are much too inclined to attach more significance to past failures than is strictly justified in rational terms. The impact of a negative experience is generally felt more strongly than the impact of a positive one.[85] If this negative experience leads to the paralysis of further action, there is a risk of becoming trapped in a downwards spiral – a spiral that must be avoided at all costs.

The psychology of the situation

TABLE 8 Take-aways for dealing with failures

Take-aways for dealing with failures

Do not encourage a negative frame of mind by focusing only on what might have been
Only thinking about what might have been invites a focus on the positive things that could have happened but did not. Such a focus makes things worse and will not help you in overcoming fear to fail.

Focus on the reasons for the lack of success and learn from it
If you understand the conditions that have led to the failure you may be better prepared in the future to deal with similar situations. Adopting such a learning approach may prepare you better and at the same time increase your confidence.

Analyse how things might have turned out even worse
An alternative way of looking at failures may be to focus on those situations that could even have been worse. The Meaning and significance of things and events in people's lives is determined by the reference points that you use to compare your current situation to. In this process, you have the choice: go for much better comparison points that make you feel worse or go for comparison points that can help you in feeling relieved that even worse outcomes were avoided. The latter is more effective in helping you to learn from the failures that you encountered.

Don't be afraid to learn from your mistakes
If you have failed or made mistakes then try to cope with it in an active manner. Too many people avoid thinking about failures because it is in contrast with the positive view they hold about themselves or they do not want to be reminded of their limited self. Such avoiding strategies aimed at maintaining your positive self-image may actually do more harm than good. Basically, it makes clear that people are afraid of being confronted with their weaker points. But, don't forget it will be the failures that allow you to grow – not so much the successes!

Be optimistic by accurately assessing the failure situation and seeing the potential of growth
Being able to face your failures and not running away from it implies that you need to foster an optimistic view on life. You have to convince yourself that even in situations of failure there can be a potential for growth. Endorsing such belief is important because it may give you the extra energy needed to engage in an accurate assessment of what happened. You can only truly learn from a failure if you can get your head around it and collect all the information needed.

It may sound strange – and it will certainly run contrary to your own hopes and expectations – but a crisis and a lack of success actually opens up some interesting possibilities (see Table 8 for a quick overview).

As a leader, you would do well to focus on these possibilities and the opportunities they present. Viewed rationally, a lack of previous success is no reason to throw your towel into the ring. And we have already seen that putting off decisions is no good to anyone. True, research does indicate that the most common reaction after failure is one in which very little in the way of constructive and cooperative behaviour can be expected.[86] In these circumstances, people often look for ways to push their responsibilities onto others.[87] In reality, this is simply another form of procrastination.

But it doesn't have to be this way. There is absolutely no reason why we should not react more forcefully and more positively to failure. The way people deal with a lack of success is largely determined by the manner in which the results are interpreted. Many people regard failure as an undesirable situation and consequently compare this undesirable situation with a situation that is less undesirable. In other words, our thoughts become focused on a situation that could have been better. By imagining in this way that success was a realistic possibility, we encourage a negative frame of mind. This negativity will continue to dominate our thinking as long as we believe that success was possible. Of course, to some extent this is a natural reaction, but it doesn't necessarily have to be a problem. On the contrary, it can even have a motivating effect, if approached in the right manner. The first step is to realise that thinking about 'what might have been' serves no useful purpose. Instead, it is important to look at reasons for the lack of success openly and honestly, so that it becomes possible to identify learning points. What could we have done differently and how? Answers to this kind of question can help to turn failure into a learning experience, allowing you to accumulate the building blocks for the construction of future success. For this reason, it is also important that leaders should analyse how things might have turned out even worse, not only to avoid these problems in the future but also to see which elements had a mitigating influence on the current situation. This will help you to work further on your strong points – because you can only fully understand your strengths when you also recognise where your weaknesses lie.

This is a key message: you should never be afraid to learn from your mistakes. People certainly dislike failure, just as they dislike uncertainty. But failure and uncertainty both exist, and we need to come to terms with them, rather than burying our heads in the sand. To ensure that leaders remain effective and continue to take decisions, it is therefore first necessary for them to face up to their mistakes. If you can succeed as a leader in putting your own lack of success into a proper perspective, you will have a much better understanding of your strengths and weaknesses. And this is the ideal breeding ground for a growing optimism on which future triumphs can be built. Identifying and feeding optimism – both your own and your followers' – is one of the most important responsibilities of a leader. Of course, it is essential that this optimism is based on actual facts that make growth and success a real possibility. Leaders who continue to preach an optimism that is built on fantasy rather than fact will do more harm than good in the long run. In contrast, optimism based on an accurate assessment of the situation acts as a valuable learning experience that can open the door on a brighter and better future.

Chapter 4
Culture, global leadership and procrastination

Delaying decisions, slacking off, not taking responsibility for difficult decisions and their potential consequences, it seems like every leader is doing it to some extent. So, does leader procrastination travel around the globe affecting many leadership practices? In other words, are there any cross-cultural differences with respect to the issue of leadership procrastination? Despite the fact that culture is a factor always to be reckoned with, many real-life cases and experiences illustrate that procrastination in our globalised world seems widely shared among our leaders. Why is this true?

Let us first take a look at the concept of culture and what it entails. The concept of culture reflects a collective mindset that influences how members of specific groups, societies and countries interpret and experience social events and behaviours. Such collective mindset emerges because individuals from different backgrounds and cultures are exposed to different traditions, heritages, rituals, customs and religions. These factors boil together to create a more or less unique set of values, beliefs and norms; consequently affecting judgements, interpretations and perceptions to a large extent. In the past, much effort has been devoted to classify countries with respect to a number of cultural dimensions, particularly so by the social scientist Geert Hofstede.[88,89] At this moment the cultural typology – as initiated by the work of Hofstede – consists of the basic dimensions of (1) power distance, (2) uncertainty avoidance, (3) individualism, (4) masculinity and (5) Confucian dynamism.

Daily mentions of leaders delaying decisions make clear that leadership worldwide is affected by procrastination tendencies. As we have seen so far, the tendency of leaders hesitating to make a decision and delaying important interventions excessively is influenced by a variety of individual and situational variables. So, although leaders worldwide

Culture, global leadership and procrastination

TABLE 9 Factors affecting procrastination as a function of the salient cultural dimension

Cultural dimension	Factors influencing procrastination
Power distance	– Desire to avoid conflicts
	– Strong feelings of distrust
Uncertainty avoidance	– Tendency to stick to the status quo
	– Neurotic leadership styles
	– Personal problems in dealing with uncertainty
Individualism	– Neurotic leadership styles
	– Not being authentic
Masculinity	– Transition to being the new leader
	– Lack of previous success
	– Regulation of one's own emotions
Confucian dynamism	– Being accountable or having little anonymity
	– Making ethical decisions

may show signs of procrastination, cultural differences may exist in the type of variable that influences their tendency to delay decisions. For example, in China a widespread belief exists that in order to save face it is very important not to make mistakes. So, if they have to make decisions and accountability is high, many Chinese people will refrain from making a decision. Their idea will be that it is better to be inactive right now rather than make a decision that could turn out wrong. In other words, some factors contributing to procrastination – as discussed in this book – may be more prevalent in some cultures compared to others. Below, I will identify which factors may be more prevalent in which type of culture. Thus, leader procrastination may be experienced everywhere, but depending on the specific cultural dimensions of the specific country, the factors determining leadership procrastination may differ (see Table 9 for an overview of the factors influencing procrastination across the different cultural dimensions).

Cultural dimensions and procrastination factors

Cultural dimension 1: Power distance

Societies are not entirely equal. Power differences exist between people, groups and companies. An important question is whether people accept such power differences or not. Do they challenge the existing power situation? If individuals accept the idea that power is distributed unequally then the culture is defined as high in power distance. Then, the existing hierarchical order is accepted and no additional justifications are needed. The idea may even exist that the inequality of power is natural and differences in privileges and endowments are legitimate. If the culture is low in power distance then people will challenge power differences and strive to distribute power in an equal manner. Differences in power will be scrutinised very carefully and justifications will be demanded for those differences to be accepted. Countries with high power distance scores include China, India, Arabic-speaking countries as well as Russia and its former satellite states.

If decisions are delayed in cultures high in power distance then two variables seem likely to contribute. The first one is the issue of *avoiding conflicts*. Depending on the power dynamics present, people may hesitate to confront others. In high power distance cultures this will be more likely the case as keeping face is very important and any instigation of conflict can be regarded as a sign of challenging the existing power hierarchy. As a result, decisions may be delayed and if taken they will be relatively poor in quality and content. In a related vein, in strong power distance cultures the idea may be very present that punctuality, wasting no time and making sure that service is provided on time is the responsibility of the subordinate. In the leader's view – in those cultures – it is the subordinate's task to take care of the responsibilities of the leader. If this is the case, it may not be a surprise that sometimes decisions are not taken at all.

The second variable relates to the issue of *distrust*. When differences in power exist between people, the interests of different parties do not overlap; rather they are different as well. Under those circumstances, it is unclear whether parties are motivated to serve each other's interests. In high power distance cultures this is less likely to be the case. As a result, distrust in each other's intentions is likely to be higher than in low power distance cultures. The presence of distrust can then be expected to distort the decision-making process in ways that little coordination, cooperation and constructive feedback will be available.

Cultural dimension 2: Uncertainty avoidance

In life many things are unpredictable and therefore cannot be controlled. How we deal with such uncertainty is reflected in the dimension of uncertainty avoidance. Hofstede defined uncertainty avoidance as 'the degree to which members of a society feel uncomfortable with uncertainty and ambiguity, leading them to support beliefs promising certainty and to maintain institutions protecting conformity' (p. 347).[90] Cultures high in uncertainty avoidance thus feel uncomfortable with uncertainty and are less willing to forego control. Therefore, they are often reluctant to actions, ideas and social changes that make things more ambiguous and less predictable. The adoption of strong laws, regulations and controls is very much endorsed. Cultures low in uncertainty avoidance, in contrast, are more relaxed about possible changes and are more willing to take risks and deal with an increase in uncertainty. Countries with high uncertainty avoidance scores include Taiwan, Germany, Greece, Portugal, Belgium and Uruguay.

When decisions are delayed in cultures high in uncertainty three variables are likely to be prominent in the decision-making process. The first variable concerns the issue of *status quo*. Leaders and organisations willing to maintain the status quo are mostly avoidant of uncertainty. They do not know what the future entails and prefer a certain (and maybe even less optimal) situation over an uncertain one. This tendency translates itself in the use of formal procedures, which slow down considerably creative and adaptive decisions.

The second variable concerns the issue of neuroticism. As we have seen earlier, leaders can display behaviours that are characteristic of neurotic leadership styles. One common aspect of those types of leaders is that their neurotic thinking style makes them averse to unclear and ambiguous situations. Those scoring high on neuroticism have problems dealing with uncertainty and will dwell continuously on possible losses of control. Under such circumstances, it will be difficult to reach a consensus with such leaders on how to tackle problems and make focused and timely decisions. The third variable concerns the issue of uncertainty itself. Being confronted with uncertainties activates a strong general tendency to procrastinate. In cultures focusing explicitly on uncertainty this tendency to procrastinate should be enhanced.

Cultural dimension 3: Individualism

Which interests matter the most? As human beings we are connected most closely to our own interests and for that reason self-interest is considered an important human motive. To some extent, people may vary in the extent to which they take the interest of others into account and even consider it equally important to their own interests. In a similar vein, cultures may differ in the extent to which individuals pursue their own interests and visions. Cultures high in individualism identify their own goals, welfare and achievements as the most important guidelines in their lives and decisions. Those cultures are characterised by interpersonal relationships that are not deeply developed. Rather, the connection to others and their organisations can be considered pretty weak and as such it is almost a given that individuals are expected to take care of themselves and their immediate families only. Cultures low in individualism, however, emphasise on group welfare and have a more collectivistic orientation when looking at their environment. They look at the world in terms of 'we' rather than 'I'. Countries with high individualism scores include the United States, the United Kingdom, Australia, France and Germany.

When cultures are highly individualistic two variables may affect leadership procrastination strongly. As with cultures high in uncertainty, *neuroticism* will also matter in highly individualistic cultures. This is not surprising as neurotic leadership types can sometimes also be classified as narcissistic people putting their own interests and reputation first. Cultures that value individual achievements in combination with neurotic behavioural displays create a fruitful environment for bad decisions.

The second variable concerns *not being authentic*. If the individual identity is much valued, survival depends to a large extent on the own achievements and as such self-knowledge is a priority. Not knowing one's own values, visions and goals may undermine the effectiveness of being ambitious and striving for the best. Leaders scoring low on authenticity in highly individualistic cultures will therefore likely produce sub-optimal decisions and ultimately fail to deliver any decision at all.

Cultural dimension 4: Masculinity

Our contemporary world and market thinking is heavily influenced by competitiveness. Notwithstanding the presence of such forces, cultures may differ in the extent to which they embrace such competitiveness as reflected in the notion of masculinity. Masculinity is defined as 'a preference for achievement, heroism, assertiveness, and material success' (p. 348).[91] In other words, masculine cultures emphasise on the importance of achievements and competition, which suggests a quite aggressive take on things to succeed. The development of close human relationships and gender equality is regarded as less important. In contrast, cultures with a feminine perspective strive more for interpersonal equality and take a distance from the masculine role model striving to control and be in power. Countries with high masculinity scores include Japan, Hungary, Austria, Venezuela, Italy and Switzerland.

In masculine cultures three variables may affect leadership procrastination strongly. The first variable concerns being the *new leader*. Those people emerging as a new leader will have to be strong in character and be able and willing to deal with aggressive settings. Most newly emerging leaders, however, need time to adjust to their newly acquired power position. They need to reassess their existing relationships within the organisation but also build new relationships with unknown and powerful others. The more time one needs to invest in these evaluation moments the more likely it will be that decisions will not be taken or even overruled by other – more ambitious and aggressive – members.

The second variable concerns *lack of previous success*. In cultures where success matters greatly, not living up to the expectations will undermine strongly one's sense of power and legitimacy. Consequently, every decision may be doubted strongly by others, making leaders afraid of actually taking one. Decisions will be evaluated again and again, leading to unnecessary procrastination.

The third variable concerns the *regulation of emotions*. The more effective leaders are in regulating their emotions the more self-confident and decisive they can be. This is most likely to be the case in cultures where negative emotions such as aggression can easily be displayed. In highly masculine cultures, not being able to regulate your emotions in effective ways may therefore become a limiting factor to your decision-making potential. Being exposed to highly achieving, aggressive and competitive habits brings those who are poor in regulating emotions out of balance. As a result, doubts will arise about one's own actions and which decision to take. Lack of self-confidence can then ultimately kill the decision-making process.

Cultural dimension 5: Confucian dynamism

Societies, groups and organisations exist and can only exist if social order remains and social contracts are honoured. Staying closely and intrinsically connected to the dominant social norms and expectations is reflected by the cultural dimension Confucian dynamism.[92] Cultures high on Confucian dynamism value social order and the existing social norms, which restrain people from complying and being respectful to authorities, not harming others and being supportive of social expectations. Individuals in such cultures exhibit a high degree of self-discipline and self-control.

Countries scoring high on Confucian dynamism include, for example, Brazil and China, whereas Western countries like the Netherlands, Sweden, Poland and Germany are in the middle range.

In cultures high on Confucian dynamism two variables may have an effect on leadership procrastination. The first variable concerns the issue of *limited anonymity*. Not being able to deal effectively with one's public image will negatively affect one's decision-making abilities. In cultures high on Confucian dynamics, skills are needed to balance one's public impressions with one's behaviours. A lack of these skills may bring to the fore the fact that one as a leader may not be able to meet the social expectations, which can even be seen as a sign of disrespect. If this is the case, then one's decisions may lack impact, making them futile in eliciting necessary changes.

The second variable concerns the issue of making *ethical decisions*. In cultures high on Confucian dynamics, the pressure is high on complying with existing social and moral expectations. As we have seen earlier, ethics is not simply a matter of objective standards but also a case of being in the 'eye of the beholder'. Individuals who do not feel merged into the existing culture endorsing the available social and moral norms will most likely experience ethical conflicts on what to do and how to do it. In their view, there will be little consensus about what is right and what is wrong. Is simply adhering to what is expected in society the only right way or do alternatives exist? For that reason, cultures with strong Confucian dynamism can be considered to some degree as morally ambivalent, where the objective and subjective perception of ethics are often at odds.

Culture and perceptions of time

From the viewpoint of a historical account cross-cultural differences seem to emerge pretty easily, particularly in how people across different regions look at the value of time. For Westerners, for example, time is costly and can't be wasted. The reason for this is that time in Western societies has become a scarce resource. We are increasingly having difficulties organising our professional and private lives because we feel that we are running out of time at every level. This is very much in contrast with how many Africans value time. For them time is not such a scarce resource. There seems plenty of it, so it cannot really be wasted. One important difference between Western and African societies is, of course, the pace of development and industrialisation. The more developed and market-dominated our lives are, the more time seems to be a scarce resource.

But, even within Western societies the different histories and attitudes towards life determine how time is looked upon. Take, for example, the difference between the French and the Americans. France used to be an aristocratic society in which physical labour was a sign of low status. This aristocratic disdain for work is still partly reflected in the attitude of the French that delaying decisions is not necessarily a bad thing, particularly so if it challenges economic exploitation and the so widely supported liberal standards of efficiency. After all, life has to be something you can enjoy at your own pace and not being dictated by time–efficiency work schedules. Procrastination as such does not necessarily need to be perceived as a social problem. This kind of thinking is very much in contrast to the views that many Americans hold. For them work achievements define who they are and fill them with pride and a sense of esteem as an individual. Their perspective is much more focused on the development as an individual and putting off things is experienced as a waste of time one should not tolerate. With this perspective in mind, it is easy to see why for Americans procrastination is a serious problem in their strive for complete fulfilment.

What science tells us?

What about science? The first observation is that research on cross-cultural differences in procrastination is limited and applications towards leadership are virtually non-existing. The studies that are out there, however, reveal inconsistent results. One study compared college students from collectivistic cultures (East Asian, Japan, Hong Kong and Thailand) with those from individualistic ones (the United States, Australia and New Zealand) and showed that overall Asian students procrastinated more.[93] Within the sample of the Asian countries it were particularly Japanese students that reported the highest procrastination-inclined scores, followed by the Taiwanese and students from Hong Kong, the United States, Australia and New Zealand. Interestingly, on the Hofstede's dimensions, Japan is a country with a strong orientation towards uncertainty avoidance. As I noted earlier, having a strong tendency to avoid *uncertainties* will most likely foster procrastination. Moreover, Japan also scores highly on the masculinity dimension, which suggests that the dominant male approach towards problems may not be effective in dealing with them, most likely because it reveals *self-control* problems that lead to a delay of decisions.

In fact, a more recent study indeed shows that males report higher levels of procrastination than females.[94] One important reason for this gender difference is that men were poorer in self-regulation than women. This study also demonstrated some cross-cultural differences. Specifically, it was found that Singaporean adolescents procrastinated more than Canadian adolescents. Singapore scores highly on the power distance dimension and this dimension is characterised by a strong preference for the *status quo* (i.e. reflected in the preference to maintain power hierarchies). As discussed in Chapter 2, leaders displaying a status quo bias are more likely to avoid responsibilities of change and thus to delay decisions and actions. Finally, a study by Joseph Ferrari and colleagues using data from six nations (Spain, Peru, Venezuela, the United Kingdom, Australia and the United States) observes no cross-cultural differences in chronic procrastination, suggesting that putting off decisions may be more prevalent across diverse populations and countries than anticipated.[95]

This latter finding underscores an important message with respect to how the presence and absence of cross-cultural differences have to be interpreted. Specifically, it is necessary to remember that the notion of culture reflects a collective mindset that is prevalent in one group (i.e. country, region, society) relative to another group. This collective mindset is a collection of values, experiences and norms that influence how members of one group look at and assign value to things in life. Important to stress, however, is that a collective mindset does not imply that all individuals of that one group will think alike. Differences will exist between individuals in a same group, society or country, making the point that across cultures people may display similar behaviours and interpret social events in similar ways. A collectivistic mindset is a proxy that can be used to categorise behavioural differences with respect to social perceptions and evaluations, but does not apply to all social behaviours out there. One such behaviour does seem to be – at least to some extent – procrastination.

CHAPTER 5

The consequences of delaying decisions

We all want to make progress. We humans are learning organisms and we have a tendency to evaluate our existence in terms of growth and profit. Finding the strength to continually improve is therefore one of the things that we look for in life. Any opportunities that present themselves must be seized with both hands. It is built into our DNA that we want to go further, faster and higher. Viewed from this perspective, it is little wonder that a failure to take decisions is equated with failure and ineffectiveness. Procrastination and avoidance are not compatible with our fundamental human instinct to keep moving forward. Leaders who are unable to satisfy this basic instinct will not be long tolerated in their role as representative of the group. If you cannot win approval and support from your followers, your career as a leader is destined to be a short one.

Procrastination can indeed lead to all kinds of unpleasant consequences for a leader, ranging from financial difficulties to career and health problems. Just as seriously, the delaying or avoidance of decisions can have far-reaching consequences for followers as well. But what exactly are these consequences?

Financial consequences

It will come as no surprise to learn that people who have difficulty in controlling their impulses often end up with financial problems. The relationship between an inability to act and negative financial consequences is clearly present in our society. A famous study conducted in Chicago provided direct proof that a tendency to procrastinate undermines your financial results.[96,97] In this study of a group of MBA students it was found that they had the possibility to win 300 dollars by playing a series of games. Once the games were over, the students were given a choice with regard to their winnings. They could either immediately receive a cheque for the 300 dollars or they could wait for two weeks, in which case they would receive a larger amount. Most of the students took the first option – immediate payment. There was nothing wrong with this, of course, but it was curious to note that these students, who wanted their money up front, then took an average of four weeks before actually cashing their cheque in the bank! If they had waited just two weeks they would have automatically got a larger sum from the test organisers, but the majority rejected this offer. This would have been a perfectly rational strategy, if they had cashed their cheque immediately, but by postponing their action they actually lost out financially!

Your financial strength can also be diminished if your career does not run as smoothly as you had hoped. In his excellent book about procrastination, Piers Steel observes that people who delay decisions or put off action are generally less successful.[98] The large majority of procrastinators (63%) perform under the average level for what can usually be regarded as a successful career. In other words, leaders who procrastinate will in general perform less well than leaders who can resist or control this temptation. For this reason, it is vital that leaders who have the opportunity to grow within an organisation are coached in a manner that helps them to understand the importance of self-control as a key element in their leadership make-up.

Another way of demonstrating that procrastinating behaviour can have serious financial consequences is to look at the costs it creates for society. Let's take, for example, the negative results of such behaviour for organisations in European countries like Belgium and the Netherlands (for organisations in the United States, see the excellent book by Piers Steel). The findings alone are staggering. If we look at the total working population in both countries and then calculate their average earnings on the basis of an eight-hour day, the figures tell a sombre story. Based on statistics for 2010, there were 7,785,000 people at work in the Netherlands, with an average gross annual salary of 34,600 euros. The average number of working hours per year was 1703 hours. The researchers estimated that for each 8-hour day, no less than 25% of the time – 2 hours per day or 414 hours each year – is spent exhibiting procrastinating behaviour. A little simple arithmetic tells us that the average gross salary per hour in the Netherlands in 2010 was 20.31 euros (34,600/1703), and that the total cost of procrastinating behaviour was therefore 8408.34 euros per employee (20.31 × 414) or 65,458,926,900 euros (8408.34 × 7,785,000) for the nation as a whole. And what of their neighbours? In Belgium in 2010 there were some 3,859,000 people in active employment, earning an average gross salary of 35,232 euros. Using the same parameters of 1703 working hours per year and 2 hours of procrastinating behaviour per day, this gives a total annual loss of a massive 33,038,905,680 euros. And in both cases, these are conservative estimates – the real costs are probably much higher.

Health

The postponement of decisions can perhaps give a feeling of relief and a short-term benefit to health, but in the long run it will have a negative effect on the physical and mental well-being of leaders. People have an automatic focus on the short term and frequently react to the feelings that they are experiencing at any given moment. In contrast, there are very few people who automatically consider their needs and wishes over the longer term. This is unfortunate, since if you find yourself trapped in the spiral of postponement and avoidance, this will ultimately lead to greater stress. Procrastinators consistently suffer from a higher incidence of colds, flu and insomnia.

Even if you postpone a decision, you cannot eliminate the tension associated with the making of that decision. The uncertainty will remain and you will continue to worry about how things will turn out in the future. There may be some initial relief, but the problem will not simply go away and will soon return to haunt you, usually in a manner that weighs far more heavily on your health and your conscience than first time around. But the consequences are not just psychological – they can also be physical. There is solid evidence to show a clear connection between procrastination and increased levels of stress.[99] If you analyse the decisions you are required to make each week, you will probably conclude that your worst feelings are not the result of the total number of decisions you are asked to make but that they have their origins in the more limited number of decisions you put off – and then worry about. This type of stress can have a damaging effect on your immune system. And if your immune system is under pressure, this can lead to sleepless nights, bad eating habits and lower levels of bodily resistance and recovery. If this is allowed to persist for any length of time, a process of escalation can lead to serious long-term harm. To make matters worse, procrastinators are not the type of people who will readily visit a doctor unless it is unavoidable – by which time the damage is often already done. In other words, they even apply their procrastination to their own health! By refusing to face up to the problem, possible remedial action is not taken, so the levels of stress and nervousness increase still further – and so the vicious downward spiral into illness – and possibly worse – continues.

Another possible consequence of procrastination is alcoholism. A build-up of postponed decisions may lead some people to seek other ways to relieve the pressure they feel. One of the most 'popular' methods of doing this is the consumption of strong drink. Because they are poor in self-regulation, procrastinators are much more likely to hit the bottle than the rest of us. This means that if they drink, they are less inclined to drink with moderation. And once they start drinking to relieve stress, they will react so impulsively and so uncontrollably that they will drink more than is good for them. This often results in alcoholism, which is not only damaging to your health but also to your relations with others. Excessive use of alcohol can lead procrastinators to behave in an increasingly aggressive and emotional manner, so that they are no longer motivated to accept their responsibilities. Conflicts develop more quickly than in normal circumstances and the means to resolve them become harder and harder to find. This tendency towards alcoholism – particularly if you are a born procrastinator – can rapidly destroy the atmosphere and team spirit in your group, so that your legitimacy as a leader is in danger of being challenged. Before long, you may even lose your right to speak on behalf of your own followers.

A less obvious consequence – but nonetheless a real possibility – is that procrastinating leaders gradually become more and more isolated and lonely. The alcohol again plays an important role, by driving people away (nobody likes a drunk), but the irritation and incomprehension caused by the constant postponing of necessary decisions is also a key factor. Very few people are willing or able to find sympathy for this dilatory approach. This again increases the likelihood of conflicts and conflicts lead to a polarisation of opinions, which force the contending parties further and further apart. Soon the leader will find himself on one side of the dividing lines and most of his followers – if not all of them – on the other side. And it hardly needs to be emphasised that loneliness and isolation are also bad for people's health. In particular, loneliness has a negative effect on self-regulation. Lonely people have more difficulty controlling their impulses. They will be inclined to drink more, eat badly and neglect proper exercise. There is also evidence that loneliness can also have harmful effects on the immune system, increase blood pressure and heighten the risk of heart disease.[100] In these circumstances, stress and depression are often just around the corner.[101] The fact that people no longer have social contacts with others influences the chemical processes that decide whether or not loneliness will have a negative effect on one's overall health. Depression is a chemical reaction that means we no longer derive pleasure from our daily activities. Everything seems pointless and this feeling simply strengthens any existing tendency towards procrastinating behaviour, in the hope that everything will seem better 'tomorrow'. Unfortunately, this is almost never the case, so the negative spiral becomes ever deeper and our reactions more desperate and panic-stricken.

To break this negative relation between procrastination and ill health, it is important to take good care of yourself in all areas of your life:

- Build healthy, lasting, genuine – and not virtual – relationships with others.
- Make sure that you get enough sleep.
- Eat healthy and take enough exercise.
- Away from your work, make sure that you do things that you enjoy doing. We all need a release valve, a chance to express ourselves and be who we really are.
- Devote enough time and attention to your intimate relationships with your partner, family and close friends.
- Try to give the things in which you believe a central place in your life.

The cost to others

Leaders who regularly postpone decisions do little to promote cohesion within the group that they lead. It is noticeable that people who are led by procrastinators often complain of feeling frustrated. In the long run, this negative emotional situation within the group will result in less constructive behaviour. This might express itself as resistance to the wishes of the leader, a withdrawal of trust or an open display of mistrust, all of which might eventually persuade some people to even leave the group.

The negative consequences for the functioning of teams and organisations stem from the fact that the implicit psychological contract

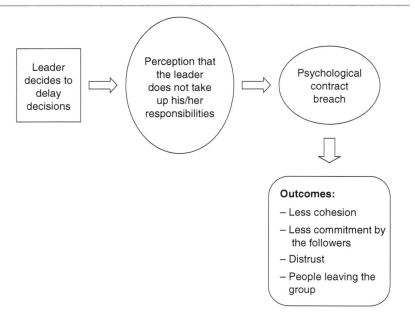

Figure 4 Social consequences of leaders' delaying decisions

between the leader and his/her followers has been broken by the leader's failure to take action (see Figure 4). This contract implies that the person who accepts the position of leader also accepts the responsibility of actively pursuing the interests of all the members of the group. It is almost as if the leader makes an unspoken promise to move the organisation forward, to the general benefit of all concerned. But there can be no progress without action and no action without decisions. Procrastinating leaders are therefore in breach of the trust given to them by their followers. The leader's promise means that the followers can reasonably assume that the leader is worthy of their trust and that he will not damage their interests.[102] They believe that the leader will feel uncomfortable and guilty if he/she does not keep his/her promises and that consequently non-compliance with the implicit or explicit agreements between the leader and the followers will weigh heavily on the leader's shoulders. This leads to the further assumption that the leader will not behave in a manner that runs contrary to his/her promise. Even so, procrastination is becoming more and more common as the years go by – certainly much more common than we would all like – and this is resulting in a growth of negative feelings in a whole range of environments.

In view of the above reasoning, it is important that leaders should be made more aware of these implicit psychological contracts with their followers. Leaders are not always fully familiar with the full range of responsibilities that they are expected to carry. This means that they will not be rationally capable of making an accurate assessment of the hopes and fears of the people they purport to represent. To allow this to become more apparent, it is necessary for leaders to create a culture of maximum transparency, where the giving and receiving of feedback is built into the DNA of the group.[103] This approach can help to ensure that the expectations of both sides – the leaders and the led – are more or less attuned to each other. In addition, it is also vital that leaders should be prepared to learn the skills and competencies that will allow them to deal with crisis situations – such as the moments when, for whatever reason, they lose their follower's trust.

As mentioned earlier in the book, every leader will display procrastinating behaviour from time to time – no one can ever eliminate it completely. The fact that this type of behaviour has a negative impact on mutual trust means that leaders must know what action they can take to win back this lost confidence – and fast. It is crucial to identify the breach of trust as soon as it occurs and to take corrective action as quickly as possible. The longer the mistrust persists, the deeper it will become. For this reason, action to restore confidence must be taken immediately and must appear spontaneous.[104] It is also important when taking this action that the leader makes clear that he/she knows why the bond of mutual trust has (temporarily) been weakened. If you admit that something has gone wrong and own up your mistakes, your followers will at least see that you understand where the root of the problem lies. Once this has been clearly communicated, the next step is to detail in an open and competent manner the steps that need to be taken to put matters right and how this will be accomplished. These points are worth repeating: you need to recognise that a breach of trust has occurred and then outline the actions that will restore that trust. Doing just one without the other will not work. If your deeds fail to match your words, you will soon acquire a reputation as an inconsistent and unreliable leader. And when this happens, you will never be able to recover your followers' lost faith in you.

Chapter 6

Leader perceptions and procrastination

So far, I have outlined the reasons why individuals in leadership positions may procrastinate and under which circumstances this is most likely to happen. As mentioned earlier, the act of procrastination may present a threat to leadership effectiveness, and viewed from that perspective delaying decisions can negatively influence the extent to which followers perceive you as a true leader. And followers' perceptions are crucial in the leadership process. Indeed, in a way we can say that what is in the eye of the beholder makes the world turn round. For example, if you are not perceived as competent, you are not competent in people's minds. The same logic applies to the issue of leadership. If you are not perceived as a leader, people will not accept your leadership. For that reason, it is extremely important to limit procrastinating behaviours as much as possible.

Important to emphasise again is the notion that delaying decisions in this book is seen as representing a leadership problem if it can be defined as irrational in nature – that is, if the procrastination behaviour is something that does not benefit anyone. In other words, when leaders delay decisions because they have no clue what to do, they are lazy or are simply not taking up responsibility. In a way their procrastination behaviour makes the leader invisible in the worst way possible. Note that sometimes delaying a decision for good reasons may, however, reveal positive benefits – even in terms of how you are perceived as a leader. In this chapter, I will specify more clearly when delaying decisions can be expected not to lead to bad outcomes but rather to reveal more efficient and positive leadership outcomes. Before moving to this issue, some more insights will be provided into why the absence – to the extent that it is possible – of procrastination can lead to more positive leadership perceptions, which eventually will lead to more support and compliance from the ones you are leading.

Leader perceptions and procrastination

TABLE 10 Positive leadership perceptions when not procrastinating

Leadership perception that you:
create strong social affiliations
have a vision
are a competent person
employ a transparent decision-making culture
are not using a strategy to serve self-interest
are a responsible person
are authentic

Several positive leadership outcomes result if one is able to reduce procrastination tendencies and behaviours (see Table 10).

Below, the outcomes as identified in Table 10 are discussed and why positive leadership perceptions are revealed is explained.

Positive leadership perceptions when not procrastinating

Leaders who are able to make decisions in a timely and accurate fashion:

- Strengthen the *social affiliations* within the company, making followers commit to the organisation and its representatives. An important ability of effective leaders is that they can foster a strong sense of identity among the ones they are leading. Leaders can be more effective if they make clear what the organisational identity is about and why it is important.[105] To do this, leaders need to make decisions in which they focus on promoting the collective welfare. Effective leadership in this case thus deals – to a certain extent – with taking action to shape a sense of identity that both leaders and followers share. From this shared sense of identity emerges the commitment that followers will display towards their leader. Making decisions that signal the commitment from the leader to the follower will further enhance this shared sense of identity. In addition, making decisions on behalf of the company and your followers also signals respect towards all organisational members, as such indicating that you are a leader that scores highly on the important leadership dimension of 'consideration'.[106,107,108]

- Make clear that they have a *vision* on how to approach problems and move the company forwards to what is needed. Effective leaders are able to point out what the problems are and in what direction the organisation has to move. Such leaders have transformational qualities and are thus able to implement change when it is needed the most. Followers who feel committed to the company will look for a leader type able to 'initiate' actions aimed at moving the company beyond the status quo (initiation).[109] Leaders who make decisions and engage in constructive action also pave the way for followers to learn. Specifically, preventing to delay decisions provides a learning moment to followers as it presents a vision that articulates where to go and what to do in order to achieve it. This way, the goals that need to and can be attained are outlined to the followers – a tactic proven to motivate people.[110] Moreover, leaders making decisions in a timely fashion also create conditions for innovation to grow. In order for teams and professionals to become innovators learning experiences are necessary. An action-driven approach by the leader will provide a fertile ground to encourage and develop followers' creative potential, making the point that innovation can be maintained and prosper in the future.[111,112]

- Show the *competence* that is expected from leaders. Making decisions when it matters the most provides the best evidence possible that you are able to make choices. It signals that you are determined to meet the expectations followers bestow on you but also that you are determined to pursue and defend your vision where necessary. This kind of motivation fuelled by competence makes for a confident and inspirational leader, which in turn enhances the trust that followers put in the leader.[113,114] It is also important to remember that making a decision holds that it is decided which options not to choose. Basically, if you decide to do one thing you also decide not to do another thing. The advantage here is that it creates less uncertainty about the road to travel as a company – too often companies get distracted because they do not know what goes and what does not go. Moreover, the ability to reduce uncertainty is strongly associated in people's mind with being a trustworthy and effective leader. This idea also aligns well with the key success of the late Steve Jobs – former CEO of Apple. He loved being focused and making things as simple as they can be, and in this process he noted: 'Deciding what not to do is as important as deciding what to do (p. 94).'[115]

- Help to create more *transparent* cultures. If decisions are delayed many times, there is little progress and hardly any achievements are made. Under such circumstances it is obviously very difficult to make progress, assess the company's strategy and make decisions on future steps to take. In fact, delaying decisions frequently creates a culture where the lack of information about achievements – there are none because decisions were not made – hinders the development of the company and its employees in several ways. First of all, because it is not clear what the outcomes will be, it becomes increasingly more difficult to understand the course of the company and what it stands for. A lack of transparency in the decision-making process emerges because the information one needs about certain decisions – that were not made – is not available, resulting in a situation where other decisions cannot be made. As a result, it becomes unclear what needs to be done and different people will start making decisions on their own will. It is not difficult to see that such conditions will not breed the future success of a company. Rather, it kills it! Second, if decisions are delayed too often, frustrations build up and after a while there are many elephants in the room that cannot be talked about. Having a culture where many things are silenced is for obvious reasons not an encouraging and constructive one. Little room will be left – the elephants take all the room – for innovative actions that can take the company forward. Subsequently, feelings of being uncomfortable will be high and eventually you will lose your best people. For those reasons, making a decision and showing the preparedness to take action is needed to eliminate a status quo situation that may eventually deteriorate in a culture that undermines the company's success and survival.

- Do not elicit the impression that they are *strategic* in their decision-making. People endorse leaders that are willing to go for the collective interest and not for their own interest. This simple idea emphasises that the legitimacy of a leader strongly depends on how intrinsically motivated people perceive him or her to be to do good for the ones he/she is leading. It is thus important to convey the message that whatever the decision made it is based on intrinsic motives and values. Unfortunately, delaying decisions almost automatically elicits inferences in people's minds that something must be going on. In other words, leaders delaying decisions can easily be blamed for being strategic. Strategy here means that the leader delays the decision to serve his/her self-interests. This kind of impression needs to be avoided. Rather, leaders being spontaneous and taking quite immediate decisions are usually perceived as being sincere – a quality strongly improving their perceived trustworthiness. Of course, a decision can be taken in spontaneous ways, but it still needs to make sense. A decision that is taken quickly and at the same time makes no sense will do no wonders to your trustworthiness. Rather, it may kill it completely as you will be seen as incompetent. The important message here is that by delaying decisions leaders too often are perceived as strategic and only motivated by more external utilitarian motives – elements that have a negative impact on leader integrity. For these reasons, it is then also important that if you have to delay decisions a clear and coherent message should be communicated why this is the case. Delaying decisions requires a transparent communication strategy. The more ambiguous and unclear your communication about your procrastination behaviour the less likely you will receive endorsement from others.

- Are being perceived as *responsible* leaders taking care of the collective good. As noted earlier, making a decision implies that you point out which direction to take but also makes clear the things that will not be done. Looking at it from this perspective, making a decision can also make you vulnerable as a leader to criticism and potential failures. As such, getting things moving signals that you are not afraid of taking responsibility for your actions, thus living up to the expectations of what a leader should do. Of course, if a decision is made that is obviously lacking inspiration and determination, followers will quickly recognise the lack of commitment on behalf of the leader and the idea of you being a responsible leader will not be on their mind. Therefore, the decision itself also needs to reflect some competence to elicit perceptions of you being a responsible decision-maker. Then, the act of making a decision will be reciprocated by followers in positive ways and create trustworthy relationships. And it is exactly those types of relationships that make those leaders who are seen as responsible shape sustainable working climates.[116]

- Create a sense of *authenticity* that provides legitimacy to future actions. The decisions that leaders take communicate what he/she stands for and believes in. Because of the existing power differences in the leader–follower relationship, followers are motivated to look for information about their leader. They are – by definition – more likely to be influenced by their leader than vice versa and therefore it is necessary to know more about the person behind the leader. Specifically, followers like to know whether the leader knows what he/she is doing and has confidence in the decisions he/she takes. Does he/she lead with the heart and has his/her priorities straight? Authentic leaders are the ones that have self-awareness, recognise their own weaknesses, strengths and the values that they believe in.[117,118] If leaders come across as authentic, followers will feel more assured that the leader will stick to his/her decisions as they are motivated by values close to his/her heart. This reassurance makes up for a trustworthy and respectful working climate. Leaders hesitating too much to make a decision, however, signal that they do not know what to do, but even more importantly that they are not sure about their own values either.

Can procrastination sometimes be a good thing?

So far, it is clear that procrastination is an important decision-making problem for many contemporary leaders. In addition, as shown above, delaying decisions too much may influence the way you are perceived as a leader in significantly negative ways. Does this mean that procrastination is never a good thing? Or, are there some benefits to delaying decisions? From an evolutionary point of view, it can be suggested that procrastination may indeed have some function in our society. If it would not have any function it would not survive and thus not be around nowadays. Of course, as illustrated in detail in this book, the true act of procrastination in a way is irrational and may actually hinder survival – read survival in this context as revealing good performance by your people leading to business success. However, human beings are by definition irrational in nature, and just like a cake without sugar does not taste well, humans also need some irrational behaviours to flourish.

In fact, many of us will probably have heard people saying that they need pressure and deadlines to perform well. These are self-proclaimed procrastinators who believe that delaying tasks and decisions will ultimately make them more creative and productive when the deadline is close. For some among us this strategy can work – they are the ones who experience low stress levels when performing.[119] Unfortunately for most of us, it does not. Many among us are not in control of our time and working with deadlines makes us stressed. So, for most of us deciding to delay action is not meant to ultimately perform better but to achieve other – more self-serving – goals like the following:

(i) Doing more enjoyable things than the job you are supposed to do
(ii) Avoiding possible failures
(iii) Avoiding performance anxiety and stress

These self-serving goals indicate that many people procrastinate out of extrinsic reasons. They hesitate to take decisions not to improve the decision-making process but rather to undermine it. That is, delaying a decision is motivated because it will bring some rewards that have little to do with doing a good job or satisfying one's own intrinsic motivations to achieve integrative and optimal solutions to the challenges they face. This observation thus clearly outlines that when leaders have to make decisions for which they can only be extrinsically motivated then procrastination will reveal major negative influences. Specifically, for tasks and decisions that leaders do not voluntarily support – they will only do those tasks because they have to – signs of delaying decisions will lead to bad or even no decision in the long run. Indeed, under those extrinsically motivated conditions, delaying decisions will then simply be a strategy aimed at avoiding execution of the job they are supposed to do. Nothing constructive will come from it.

On the other hand, if leaders are intrinsically motivated to take a decision then procrastination can be constructive. Under these circumstances, leaders have heart for the problem they are challenged with and they want to address it. This is an important difference. Because they want to face the challenge – and not because they have to – they will be more motivated to actually deliver a solution or a response. The task at hand or the decision they have to take matters to them in an intrinsic way, so they will be motivated to make the best decision possible. If this is the case, then procrastination may actually be seen as a more constructive approach. There is nothing wrong with leaders who are intrinsically motivated to be part of the solution to take some time to reflect upon it. In fact, research shows that people who like their job and are motivated to solve complex problems (e.g. NASA scientists and engineers in the case of the study) actually became more innovative when they were working with deadlines.[120] These deadlines, however,

TABLE 11 The bad and good of procrastination

When procrastination is bad
- The decision-maker has fear to make a decision
- The decision-maker is strategic
- The decision-maker is extrinsically motivated

When procrastination is good
- The decision-maker is anticipating to make a decision
- The decision-maker is constructive
- The decision-maker is intrinsically motivated

---

had to be reasonable. Further evidence also shows that when people have to make decisions about things that matter to them, that is, their values and ethics, then delaying the decision had a positive effect. When decisions deal with one's own intrinsic values, then procrastination may actually help you to make better and more ethical decisions.[121]

Taken together, under certain circumstances, delaying a decision and reflecting upon it may indeed have positive effects, but then only if specific conditions are present (see Table 11).

Chapter 7

An interactive model

So far, we have taken a journey that has allowed us to map out and explore one of the most important of current leadership problems: the postponement and avoidance of decisions, otherwise known as procrastination. This type of indecisive behaviour is the result both of factors specific to the individual leader and of factors inherent in the leadership situation. Scientific psychological research has shown that human behaviour is determined by the interaction between individual characteristics and the circumstances to which those characteristics are subjected.[122] The nature of the interaction determines the nature of the behaviour. This same reasoning can be used to explain why leaders so often procrastinate.

In this chapter we will use an interactive model to explain the why and the how of our leaders' procrastination (see Figure 5). The 'how' relates to the reasons and influences that naturally incline leaders towards the tendency to delay or avoid decisions. The 'why' relates to the factors that can have a negative impact on both the individual and situational characteristics inherent in a particular decision-making process. We need to map out these influences and factors, since they are vital to an understanding of the seemingly irrational behaviour that our leaders sometimes display. It is equally important in terms of providing our leaders with a more reliable framework for action, based on these insights. Understanding why people behave the way they do is a core condition for providing training and coaching aimed at the development of more effective and more sustainable leadership.

Specifically, knowing which factors particularly influence procrastination behaviour it should be possible to outline steps that companies and collectives can undertake to reduce leaders' procrastination. This can be done by reshaping certain working conditions that are known to facilitate procrastination and by testing (future) leaders more thoroughly on the individual factors that are known to be related to leader procrastination. Undertaking such steps requires, of course, a deeper understanding of what causes what and why it causes this. Adopting

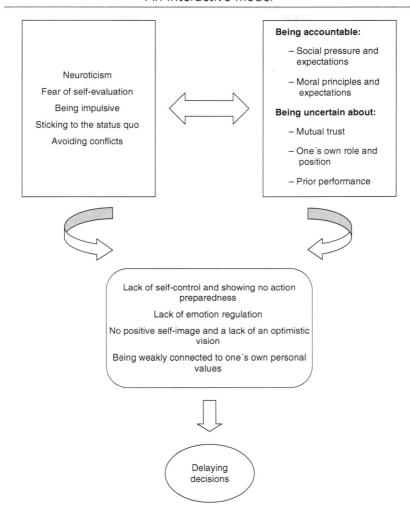

Figure 5 An interactive model

such an analytic approach therefore requires more than only the collaboration of the leader under scrutiny. It also invites the broader social context to participate in the process of shaping the organisational culture in such a way that the focus is on outlining both the social and personal factors that could stimulate or inhibit leader procrastination. In other words, in solving the problem of leader procrastination the responsibility does not only lie with the leader alone but also with those able to make higher-level decisions in the company.

The 'how' of delaying decisions

The extent to which leaders delay or avoid decisions is therefore determined by both intrinsic (inherent in the leader) and extrinsic (inherent in the situation) influences.

The *intrinsic* influences are variables that relate to the feelings and motives experienced by the leader as part of his/her personality. To a significant degree they act as a compass, prompting the leader to react to the need for action and decisions in a manner that does most to satisfy these feelings (usually of anxiety) and motives. The more fears and internal conflicts a leader experiences in his/her own mind, the more likely that his/her self-regulation will be focused on avoidance behaviour, which might ultimately include the postponement of decisions.

In particular, leaders with the following personal characteristics are more likely to demonstrate inefficient forms of self-regulation:

- Those who have a great fear of being judged by others. Their knowledge of their own strengths and weaknesses makes these leaders excessively nervous, which can activate strong inhibition behaviour. They are particularly keen to avoid moments of evaluation. Running parallel with this, they will develop an attitude that is focused on keeping everything under control, with an exaggerated attention to detail. They slow down their own action and the decision-making process through their own neurotic impulses.

- Related to these fears, they are also strongly motivated to avoid conflicts by pushing potentially contentious decisions into the future. Unfortunately, leaders often need to be firm and decisive, if they want to ensure that action beneficial to the group as a whole is taken. This means that occasional conflict is a normal part, perhaps even an indispensable part, of every leader's experience. A desire to avoid conflict will therefore result in less progress being made towards the collective objectives of the group. In other words, procrastination creates a very strong status quo bias.

- In order to keep the peace and avoid being evaluated, leaders can also sometimes display inconsistent and unpredictable behaviour, where they jump from one extreme to the other in an effort to avoid being pinned down. Avoiding a firm choice between different options or switching indiscriminately from one option to another can sometimes mean that 'everything' is seen as being potentially interesting, so that 'nothing' – or very little – ultimately gets done. This strategy leads to inconsistent policy with frequent changes of direction and does not lead to sustainable long-term development. As a consequence, the conflicts that the leader was trying to avoid will happen anyway, and questions will be asked about the effectiveness of his/her leadership role.

For companies it is important to determine early on in the recruitment process of future leaders or in the guidance of high potentials whether these individuals display these kinds of behaviours or have the potential to develop these tendencies in the future. To prevent or manage these individual psychological processes, it is necessary to organise learning trajectories where these processes are dealt with. What to do in these trajectories? Because the psychological tendencies discussed above are strongly related to self-control activities, it will be important to provide these individuals with a stronger sense of being in control at the job and in their role as leader. Specifically, many of the processes related to the fear of being evaluated, to avoid conflicts and maintaining the status quo and trying to please everyone to the detriment of one's own consistent leadership style hold that these leader types are focused too much on the details of the job and act more as immediate problem solvers rather than as leaders with a grand vision able to transform and change companies. For this reason it is important to ensure that the company is helping these leaders to move from being a player on the work floor who is merged into all the relational and task details to a leader who is[123]:

- *A generalist:* someone who has a more overall view of what is happening within the company and knows how to align all that is going on with the goals that the company endorses To achieve this mindset it is required that these leaders learn to develop a viewpoint that is rooted in the company's strategy and translated into specific actions to take. In other words, leaders will have to develop decision-making templates based on a more general view of the company's objectives.
- *An integrator:* someone who has the big picture in mind but at the same time is also able to see how all the different parts fit together. Both micro and macro management join forces in this perspective. It allows one to be able to understand the specific

needs of relationships within the company and align them with the general objective. Having an integrative mindset is strongly related to creative personalities fostering innovation.

- *A catalyst of change:* someone who understands that status quo thinking is not accepted when it is motivated by a conservative mindset. Leadership entails the quality to transform existing social collectives into new and adaptive ones. This is necessary when situations change and new challenges are encountered. Of course, if the status quo is the most optimal one, this kind of leader will then stick to the existing situation, but from the viewpoint it is necessary for adaptive reasons and not out of fear to change anything.

The *extrinsic* influences are variables that relate to the situation in which the leader finds himself/herself. The leader will not make a conscious choice in respect of these influences, because they are inherent – and therefore often unseen – in the development of the specific circumstances. Of course, it is perfectly possible that a certain type of leader will unconsciously feel attracted to a certain type of situation – situations in which they feel more comfortable than others. But on the other hand, it is also true that leaders often do not have a choice about the situations in which they find themselves placed. Some situations just happen – and need to be dealt with. The impact of the situation is to be found in its capacity to strengthen particular motives and tendencies in the personality of the leader, thereby increasing the influence of these motives and tendencies on his/her actions (or lack of them). If the tendencies and motives are positive and facilitating, the effect on the leader's behaviour will be beneficial. If the tendencies and motives are negative and inhibitive, the effect on the leader's behaviour will be detrimental.

For situations characterised by the following features, there is a good chance that leaders who display the individual personality traits outlined above will be more likely to display even greater levels of procrastination:

- Situations can differ in the extent to which the leader is likely to be evaluated publicly. Actions and decisions that need to be taken in the presence of others or under the spotlight of publicity will only serve to strengthen any existing fears for evaluation that the leader may have. In cases of this kind, it is important to make sure that the decision is thoroughly prepared before it is made public. When people experience social pressure, moral issues very quickly rise to the surface. In other words, each decision will be viewed and assessed from a moral perspective. This means that it is necessary to gather sufficient information with regard to the moral principle(s) that is (are) important to your followers. Situations which are dominated by a high level of moral expectation will inevitably exercise a strong influence on the decisions that are eventually taken.

- Unfortunately, many situations are not capable of careful advance preparation. In these circumstances, the need to make a decision is surrounded by uncertainty. The greater the ambiguity of the situation, the greater the likelihood that the leader will try to procrastinate. This ambiguity can manifest itself in a number of different ways. Leaders might be uncertain about the extent to which their followers trust them, or about the manner in which their leadership is viewed, or about the extent to which their past actions may be used against them. The same uncertainty applies to the strategies likely to be used by others (who may be your opponents). The key is to do everything feasible to remove or diminish ambiguity by collecting and collating as much information as possible.

The 'why' of delaying decisions

The above factors each exercise a unique but also combined influences on the extent to which leaders are prepared to take decisions. Which processes activate these factors? And which processes ensure that both individual characteristics and situational characteristics can have an impact on the postponement and/or avoidance of decisions? The basic processes which are generally accepted to be experienced by procrastinating leaders – and therefore have a telling effect on their behaviour – operate on the following three dimensions.

Leaders who postpone or avoid decisions will have:

- Difficulty in controlling their own impulses and feelings. They will find it hard to pursue a consistent policy if they are required to take direct personal action. Their emotions (fear, anticipated regret and guilt) are experienced with great intensity and colour their perceptions about the things that they are responsible for and the things that they are not. This can lead to blindness for some of their most crucial weaknesses and to an unwillingness to meet what others see as their obligations. This results in a characteristic feeling of panic and chaos when self-regulation is necessary.

- A fairly negative self-image. The lack of self-confidence leads them to question almost everything, which simply serves to heighten their fear and neurotic behaviour. Low self-esteem means low levels of optimism, which often translates into a feeling of uselessness and an undervaluation of the importance and necessity of their own actions.

- An imperfect understanding of their own values. Feelings of doubt are closely associated with procrastinating behaviour and are engendered by a lack of self-knowledge. Not knowing what you really stand for results in a low sense of personal authenticity and a reduced capacity to react decisively and consistently to changing circumstances.

Understanding the specific processes that cause leaders to procrastinate because of their personalities and/or the situation they find themselves in can help the organisation as a whole to provide support in specific ways. These are the ways leaders manage their emotions, look at themselves and experience a sense of authenticity. If companies can provide help and support to leaders to deal in a better and more optimal way with these areas, the processes leading to procrastination can be tackled in an earlier stage. In fact, it is important that leaders are encouraged to reflect upon their past behaviours and in which context they were displayed to develop into better decision-makers. Creating a supportive working environment in which after-events reviews take place is part of successful leadership development programmes.[124] For that reason it is important that leaders:

- Receive insights into the emotions that they experience at work and why they experience them. Understanding why you experience certain emotions can already help to analyse the work situation at hand and what exactly is happening that causes these emotions to influence you. If what is happening is negatively influencing your role as a leader then the first step to take is to deal with the underlying conflicts and causes and to understand that in a way they are unrelated to many of the decisions that you will have to take on behalf of the company. Essentially, getting to know your emotional life can help to distinguish your leadership responsibilities from the things that are nagging you and basically blur your vision on what needs to be done first.

- Build on a positive self-view when taking up their leadership role. It is essential that not only negative feedback or high expectations are communicated that put people under stress. People at leadership positions understand the relevance of their position within the organisation and are usually motivated to do a good job. Too often, however, this positive view on leadership is undermined by organisational cultures focusing too much on what could have been done better or expecting only an increase in performances. It is imperative to understand that almost any strategy has its limitations and that exactly at the moment that those limitations are experienced leadership is needed to transform or divert the company into new directions. To achieve such accomplishments it is necessary that a realistic point of view is used towards evaluating those in leadership roles.

- Recognise what they stand for and how it fits or does not fit with the corporate culture. It is essential that both the leader and company create a working situation allowing the values of both parties to be recognised and valued. True authentic leadership resides well in supportive environments that wish to foster agreements based on mutual understanding and respect rather than competitive incentives.

CHAPTER 8
What to do?

It is clear by now that delaying decisions is caused by a complex interaction of a variety of variables. To a certain degree, it will almost be impossible for leaders to completely escape the tendency to procrastinate. It is a common fact that from time to time leaders will procrastinate. What is really important, however, is that we are able to coach our leaders in such ways that they can make decisions under the best circumstances possible. These should be circumstances that can help to reduce the tendency to delay decisions. To identify such circumstances we will make use of all the insights that we have gathered so far. Based on this knowledge we will define five principles that can help to battle leaders' procrastination (see Table 12).

Principle 1: Never seek to justify procrastination

If you decide not to do certain things, then you need to justify your inaction. In general, people are fairly creative when it comes to finding such justifications. We are very good at convincing ourselves that we have the best of intentions but that on this occasion 'circumstances' have conspired against us. It is simply part of human nature to attribute our difficulties to external factors, rather than to blame our own motives and personal qualities. This means that when we begin to sense that we would prefer not to take a particular decision, we very quickly come up with an excuse to explain our inertia. If you gradually come to realise that you are in the habit of putting off decisions in this manner, then it is important that you should also realise that you need to make a serious effort to change the way you view and assess factual matters. Your perception is flawed – and you need to put it right. In all probability, the way you look at a situation is biased in a manner that allows you to continue postponing decisions. You need

What to do?

> ### TABLE 12 Principles to beat procrastination
>
> **Principle 1: Never seek to justify procrastination**
> - People are intrinsically – and automatically – motivated to attribute difficulties to external circumstances and not to their own actions.
> - It is important that you keep an open view to your responsibilities and be aware to recognise your own weaknesses.
>
> **Principle 2: Eliminate uncertainties – as far as possible**
> - Make clear what your priorities are and use those priorities as reference points to evaluate each and new subsequent decision.
> - It is important to keep focused on what you need to do as it will enable you to exclude the emergence of additional uncertainties in your decision-making process.
>
> **Principle 3: Avoid physical and mental exhaustion**
> - The lack of energy makes that your decision will be less than optimal. Having no energy leads to situations of decision delay.
> - As a leader you are responsible to identify for yourself the times and places when you feel most energetic.
>
> **Principle 4: Work at your relationships**
> - An important responsibility of leaders is also to create open climates where trust is very much present. A supportive working climate aids the process of decision-making and execution.
> - This relational task is best not done alone. Trustworthy climates are being built together!
>
> **Principle 5: Be aware of the consequences of your decisions**
> - Leaders have to anticipate the consequences of each of their decisions and analyse the situation to be prepared for what may be coming.
> - Being prepared helps you to increase your confidence with respect to the decisions you have to take and will reduce procrastination.

to do your utmost to resist this temptation. The following tips may help you:

- Be realistic! Dare to face up to the fact that the reasons why you fail to take certain decisions are to be found in your own personal shortcomings. Your vanity and your defensive way of thinking help you to justify your procrastinating behaviour. Yet by postponing decisions the situation actually becomes worse in the long run. Try to confront your own fears and put them in their proper perspective.
- Try to meet your deadlines. Keep on reminding yourself why the deadlines are there and why the task is so important. As an added motivation, make a deal with yourself to reward yourself if you

resist the temptation to procrastinate. And make sure that you do it: don't put this off to the future as well!

- Try to prepare your decisions as fully as possible. Make different scenarios and try to work out all the different consequences. What might happen if you take the decision? What might happen if you don't take the decision? It is important that you develop a spontaneous reaction in favour of making a decision – particularly if you are under pressure and would prefer not to act.
- Make clear to yourself the positive things that might be achieved if you have the courage to make the decision. Focus on the likely positive outcomes – and not on the negative ones.
- Be prepared to discuss all the responsibilities relating to the decision-making process with those around you. The feeling that you have worked together to reach a decision will give you more confidence to act.
- And, as far as possible, make sure that you do indeed act. Decisions without action are meaningless. It is important to create conditions in which you feel that you are making progress. This 'flow' can give you energy and help you to better resist the influences that can encourage procrastination.

Principle 2: Eliminate uncertainties – as far as possible

The more uncertainty you experience, the more likely you are to want to run away from a situation. The same applies to decisions: the more doubts that surround the situation, the less likely you are to want to act. For this reason, it is important to try and remove as many of these doubts and uncertainties as possible. Leaders can experience doubts and uncertainties in many different areas. For example, they can be unsure about the objectives to be reached, or what the consequences of reaching those objectives might be, or what strategy needs to be followed once the objectives have been reached. To eliminate – or at least significantly limit – these potentially paralysing problems, you can try the following:

- Make clear to yourself and to those around you precisely what steps need to be taken. What are you planning to do and what are you hoping to achieve by these actions? Once this is fully understood, agree on specific practical measures.

- Make sure that the most important priorities are also fully clear to all concerned. You cannot afford any lack of clarity or certainty about these matters. If nobody knows what your key objectives are, you are unlikely to achieve them. Your priorities will help you to remain concentrated on the 'big picture'.

- Keep your focus. Do not allow yourself to be sidetracked or distracted by things that do not bring you any nearer to your goal. Throughout the entire decision-making and implementation trajectory, you must keep your eyes fixed firmly on your final destination. If you don't know where you want to go, you are never going to get there. A clear focus will allow you to map out and record each small step of your journey, ensuring that you remain on course at all times and removing any possible need for postponement or delay.

- Identify and name any problems that may arise in a clear fashion, so that everyone knows exactly what is going on. Transparent communication can eliminate the uncertainties that lead to misunderstandings.

- Continue to ask yourself why you are doing what you are doing. If you cannot give yourself a clear answer to this question, there is a strong likelihood that you are failing to see certain crucial matters and that you are not focusing properly on the things that really need to be achieved. If this kind of ambiguity is allowed to grow, it will lead to uncertainty – and uncertainty will lead to procrastination.

Principle 3: Avoid physical and mental exhaustion

If you are no longer in a condition to maintain a rational overview of the situation, so that you are forced to rely on your impulses, this will quickly lead to procrastinating behaviour. Worse still, if you cannot concentrate or are always feeling tired, the likelihood of this behaviour will increase still further. Your physical and mental condition therefore determines to a large extent your ability to remain in control – and carry on taking decisions. For this reason, it is important to do everything necessary to prevent yourself from becoming exhausted. In this context, the following measures may be useful:

- Identify and respect your own limits. During which parts of the day do you have most energy? When are you best able to concentrate? These are the moments when you should make your decisions.

As you might expect, these moments vary from person to person. Map out your own energy patterns and follow the guidance they give you. Some of us are morning people and some of us are night owls.

- Find ways to encourage yourself to finish off tasks and complete decisions. Make a list of the things that make you happy and motivate you most effectively, and relate these things to the decisions you have to take. Striving to achieve things you want to possess or experience always gives you extra energy – and extra energy will reduce the prospect that you will need to resort to delay or avoidance tactics.
- Make sure that you get enough rest and relaxation. Take regular breaks during the day and always try to get a good night's sleep. It is important that these activities should clear your mind of any possible worries and doubts. You do not need to cram everything into your head and your brain does not need to be constantly ticking over. Knowledge sometimes goes a lot further in a fresh mind.
- Regard the decision you need to make as an opportunity rather than an obstacle. Obstacles consume energy and lead to delay. Opportunities give energy and encourage action.
- Convince yourself that you want to take the decision, rather than being 'forced' to take it. If the desire to act comes from within yourself, your motivation will be greater, as will your willingness to devote extra energy to the task in hand.

Principle 4: Work at your relationships

If you need to make decisions, the existence of conflicts and/or feelings of distrust will make things much more difficult than would otherwise be the case. They act as major irritations, which force people to adopt a defensive attitude that is not conducive to decisive action. Leaders who do not have good relations with those around them will eventually find themselves in a position where they do not want to or are not able to take decisions. For this reason, one of the leaders' most important tasks is to maintain a good relational climate in his/her immediate environment. Your relationships with your followers must be a blessing, not a burden. To achieve this, make sure you focus on the following relational aspects:

- Gather a supportive group of people around you. Develop a circle of close friends and associates with whom you can share and test opinions, without risking any loss of face. It is important to prepare your decisions in a healthy and positive environment, but make sure that this environment does not degenerate into a kind of 'follow-my-leader' thinking. It is your task as leader to promote honesty and openness in a setting where different opinions can be exchanged frankly and freely.

- Don't try to do everything by yourself. You can only win trust if you first give trust to others. One way to build up trust is by delegating responsibilities and showing that you have confidence in the abilities of your followers to do what is necessary. This will also allow you to devote more time to the 'big picture' and to the further improvement of key relationships.
- Create a climate in which potential conflicts can be talked out in a constructive manner. Do not wait until these conflicts are almost at a bursting point. When matters have gone this far, the relationship often becomes so sour that everyone seeks to avoid a reconciliation, so that corrective action is no longer possible. In these circumstances, procrastination is almost certain to follow.

Principle 5: Be aware of the consequences of your decisions

One of the problems of making decisions is that their consequences can sometimes seem so dramatic and so overwhelming. This is a factor that suddenly causes many leaders to get cold feet – and so they postpone action or delay it indefinitely. It is therefore important to have a clear and accurate focus on the likely outcome of your decision and the effects that it will have on both yourself and others. This will also help you to take a more well-considered decision, since it will encourage you to look at various different scenarios and their probable impact. This will give you greater self-awareness and self-confidence as you approach the decision-making process. In addition, a sharp focus on possible consequences will mean that you are less likely to be intimidated by the things that can go wrong. The fact that a leader is expected to bear a heavy responsibility can sometimes have a paralysing effect on his/her actions. In these circumstances, every outcome – no matter how big or small – can feel like a ton weight, pressing down on the leader's shoulders. This burden can be reduced if you face up to the prospect of potential problems and failure and plan in advance what you will do if this eventuality arises.

If a decision is being taken one thus needs to be prepared in terms of the consequences that may happen. One needs to know the consequences of one's decisions because:

- It does not help to delay decisions. For this reason it is best that you know in advance all the possible consequences that may happen. Delaying decisions will in the long term lead to situations that are unsustainable. Doing nothing is worse than actually doing something and therefore it is advised that you run through all the possible consequences that may occur. It can help you to be better prepared towards the future and prevent you from getting stuck in a spiral of indecision that will undermine your preparation about what could happen.

CHAPTER 9

The 'Leadership on Hold' – Survey©

Procrastination is irrational! It may be comfortable in the short term but it is destructive in the long term. The aim of this book is to provide insights into why leaders delay decisions. Knowing why can help you as a leader to identify your own hesitations, to explain it and hopefully eliminate it. To do this, first of all, you need to be aware whether or not you have a habit of delaying decisions. To facilitate this task I have developed the 'Leadership on Hold' (LH)-survey (© Dr. David De Cremer). This survey allows you to identify whether (a) you score high on individual factors that can determine whether you delay decisions or not, and (b) you have to make decisions within a context that facilitates delaying decisions. To achieve this purpose the survey consists of two parts. In the first part we look at the degree to which you have an innate inclination to delay decisions (referred to as *the individual*) whereas in the second part (referred to as the context) we look at whether specific circumstances are present that can facilitate delay of decisions.

Each part of this survey presents a series of statements. For each statement you are required to indicate on a 7-point scale whether you agree with the statement or not.

1 = *totally inapplicable to me*
2 = *not applicable to me*
3 = *not really applicable to me*
4 = *neutral*
5 = *slightly applicable to me*
6 = *applicable to me*
7 = *fully applicable to me*

Part 1: The individual

In this part of the survey we look at the extent to which you are inclined to delay decisions. How to interpret your scores? In total you will be presented with 12 statements (total points = 84). To know your total score you need to add all your scores for each of the statements. If your total score is higher than the average score (= 42 points) then chances are high that you will delay decisions more. If your score is lower than the average score then you will be less inclined to delay decisions.

I am someone who...

Experiences doubts with every decision I take

1	2	3	4	5	6	7

Engages in self-handicapping strategies to justify possible failures in an easy way

1	2	3	4	5	6	7

Does not feel comfortable when I have to make a decision

1	2	3	4	5	6	7

Does not like to change from one environment to another

1	2	3	4	5	6	7

Would not change an existing situation very quickly

1	2	3	4	5	6	7

The 'Leadership on Hold' – Survey©

Likes to avoid conflicts if possible

1	2	3	4	5	6	7

Does not find it easy to talk about differences in opinion

1	2	3	4	5	6	7

Does not like to be evaluated by others

1	2	3	4	5	6	7

Analyses all alternatives very (even too) carefully before taking a decision

1	2	3	4	5	6	7

Takes decisions very spontaneously

1	2	3	4	5	6	7

Does not think too much before taking a decision

1	2	3	4	5	6	7

Allows my emotions to influence my decisions

1	2	3	4	5	6	7

Part 2: The context

In this part of the survey we look at the extent to which the context surrounding your decisions has specific features that may facilitate procrastination. Again, you will be presented with 12 statements (total points = 84). To know your total score you need to add all your scores for each of the statements. If your total score is higher than the average score (= 42 points) then you should be aware that the context will most likely facilitate delay of decisions. If your score is lower than the average score then the context is less likely to influence the emergence of procrastination.

I have to make a decision in a context…

That is very important for my future career

1	2	3	4	5	6	7

In which my behaviour is evaluated on moral grounds

1	2	3	4	5	6	7

Where my personal and collective interests are at odds

1	2	3	4	5	6	7

That is unclear about what the 'big picture' is

1	2	3	4	5	6	7

That is characterised by a climate of distrust

1	2	3	4	5	6	7

The 'Leadership on Hold' – Survey©

That is characterised by fear to evoke conflicts

1	2	3	4	5	6	7

Where others will evaluate me

1	2	3	4	5	6	7

In which others know the kind of decision I have to make

1	2	3	4	5	6	7

That is unclear about the goals that have to be achieved

1	2	3	4	5	6	7

That includes so many details that it makes unclear the priorities I have to achieve

1	2	3	4	5	6	7

Takes so much energy out of me that I cannot sleep

1	2	3	4	5	6	7

That makes it difficult for me to keep an overview of all the things that I have to do

1	2	3	4	5	6	7

References

1. Haines, S. (2009). Bankrupt leadership development? *Training, 64,* 64.
2. De Cremer, D., Mayer, D. M., Van Dijke, M., Schouten, B. C., & Bardes, M. (2009). Self-sacrificial leadership promoting prosocial behavior: The moderating role of prevention focus. *Journal of Applied Psychology, 94,* 887–899.
3. Van Knippenberg, D., & Hogg, M. A. (2003). A social identity model of leadership effectiveness in organizations. *Research in Organizational Behavior, 25,* 243–295.
4. Lewin, K., Lippitt, R., & White, R. K. (1939). Patterns of aggressive behavior in experimentally created social groups. *The Journal of Social Psychology, 10,* 271–299.
5. Taggar, S., Hackew, R., & Saha, S. (1999). Leadership emergence in autonomous work teams: Antecedents and outcomes. *Personnel Psychology, 4,* 899–926.
6. De Cremer, D. (2012). Leaders need a lesson in crisis management. *Financial Times*, 23 January.
7. Hogan, R., Curby, G., & Hogan, J. (1994). What we know about leadership effectiveness and personality. *American Psychologist, 6,* 493–504.
8. House, R. J. (1996). Path-goal theory of leadership. Lessons, legacy, and a reformulated theory. *The Leadership Quarterly, 7,* 323–352.
9. Vroom, V. H., & Yetton, P. W. (1973). *Leadership and decision making*. Pittsburgh, PA: University of Pittsburgh Press.
10. Stogdill, R. M., & Cooms, A. E. (1957). *Leader behavior: Its description and measurement*. Columbus: Bureau of Business Research.
11. Whetton, D. A., & Cameron, K. S. (2002). *Developing management skills* (5th edition). Upper Saddle River: Prentice Hall.
12. Kotter, J. P. (1995). Leading change: Why transformation efforts fail. *Harvard Business Review, 73,* 59–67.
13. Bass, B. M. (1998). *Transformational leadership: Industry, military, and educational impact*. Mahwah, NJ: Erlbaum.

References

14. De Cremer, D. (2002). Charismatic leadership and cooperation in social dilemmas: A matter of transforming motives? *Journal of Applied Social Psychology, 32,* 997–1016.
15. Shamir, B., Zakay, E., Breinin, E., & Popper, M. (1998). Correlates of charismatic leader behavior in military units: Subordinates' attitudes, unit characteristics, and superiors' appraisals of leader performance. *Academy of Management Journal, 41,* 387–409.
16. De Cremer, D., & van Knippenberg, D. (2004). Charismatic leadership, collective identification, and leadership effectiveness: The interactive effects of leader self-sacrifice and self-confidence. *Organizational Behavior and Human Decision Processes, 95,* 140–155.
17. De Cremer, D., van Dick, R., Tenbrunsel, A. E., Pillutla, M., & Murnighan, J. K. (2011). Understanding ethical behaviour and decision making in management: A behavioural business ethics approach. *British Journal of Management, 22,* 1–4.
18. Giuliani, R. W. (2002). *Leiderschap*. Utrecht: Het Spectrum.
19. Lewin, K., Lippitt, R., & White, R. K. (1939). Patterns of aggressive behavior in experimentally created social groups. *The Journal of Social Psychology, 10,* 271–299.
20. De Cremer, D., & Tyler, T. R. (2005). Managing group behavior: The interplay between procedural fairness, self, and cooperation. In M. Zanna (Ed.), *Advances in experimental social psychology* (Vol. 37, pp.151–218). New York: Academic Press.
21. Peterson, R. S. (1997). A directive leadership style in group decision making can be both virtue and vice: Evidence from elite and experimental groups. *Journal of Personality and Social Psychology, 72,* 1107–1121.
22. De Cremer, D. & Tenbrunsel, A. E. (2011). *Behavioral business ethics: Shaping an emerging field*. New York: Taylor & Francis.
23. De Cremer, D., Zeelenberg. M., & Murnighan, J. K. (Eds., 2006). *Social psychology and economics*. Mahwah, New Jersey: Lawrence Erlbaum Association.
24. Kahneman, D. (2011). *Thinking, fast and slow*. London: Penguin books.
25. Steel, P. (2011). *The procrastination equation*. Edingburgh: Pearson Education Limited.
26. Baumeister, R. F., & Thierney, J. (2011). *Willpower: Rediscovering the greatest human strength* (p. 24). Penguin Press HC.
27. Steel, P. (2007). The nature of procrastination: A meta-analytic and theoretical review of quintessential self-regulatory failure. *Psychological Bulletin, 133,* 65–94.

28. Steel, P. (2011). *The procrastination equation*. Edingburgh: Pearson Education Limited.
29. Sabini, J., & Silver, M. (1982). *Moralities of everyday life*. Oxford: Oxford University Press.
30. Grondin, S. (2001). From physical time to the first and second moments of psychological time. *Psychological Bulletin, 127,* 22–44.
31. Keough, K. A., Zimbardo, P. G., & Boyd, J. N. (1999). Who's smoking, drinking, and using drugs? Time perspective as a predictor of substance use. *Basic and Applied Social Psychology, 21,* 149–164.
32. Kahneman, D., & Tversky, A. (1981). The framing of decisions and the psychology of choice. *Science, 211,* 453–458.
33. Buehler, R., Griffin, D., & Ross, M. (2002). Inside the planning fallacy: The causes and consequences of optimistic time predictions. In T. Gilovich, D. Griffin, & D. Kahneman (Eds.), *Heuristics and biases: The psychology of intuitive judgment* (pp. 250–270). Cambridge, UK: Cambridge University Press.
34. Roese, N. J., & Summerville, A. (2005). What we regret most…and why. *Personality and Social Psychology Bulletin, 31,* 1273–1285.
35. Kuhl, J., & Beckmann, J. (1994). *Volition and personality: Action vs. state orientation*. Gottingen, Germany: Hogrefe.
36. Kuhl, J. (2000). A functional-design approach to motivation and volition: The dynamics of personality systems interactions. In M. Boekaerts, P. R. Pintrich, & M. Zeidner (Eds.), *Self-regulation: Directions and challenges for future research* (pp. 111–169). New York: Academic Press.
37. Koole, S. L., & Coenen, L. H. (2007). Implicit self and affect regulation: Effects of action orientation and subliminal self priming in an affective priming task. *Self and Identity, 6,* 118–136.
38. Koole, S. L., & Jostmann, N. (2004). Getting a grip on your feelings: Effects of action orientation and external demands on intuitive affect regulation. *Journal of Personality and Social Psychology, 87,* 974–990.
39. Kuhl, J. (1981). Motivational and functional helplessness: The moderating effect of state versus action orientation. *Journal of Personality and Social Psychology, 40,* 155–170.
40. Hagger, M. S., Wood, C., Stiff, C., & Chatzisarantis, N. L. D. (2010). Ego depletion and the strength model of self-control: A meta-analysis. *Psychological Bulletin, 136,* 495–525.
41. DeWall, C. N., Baumeister, R. F., Gailliot, M. T., & Maner, J. K. (2008). Depletion makes the heart grow less helpful: Helping as a function of self-regulatory energy and genetic relatedness. *Personality and Social Psychology Bulletin, 34,* 1653–1662.

References

42. Gino, F., Schweitzer, M. E., Mead, N. L., & Ariely, D. (2011). Unable to resist temptation: How self-control depletion promotes unethical behavior. *Organizational Behavior and Human Decision Processes, 115,* 191–203.
43. Muraven, M., & Baumeister, R. F. (2000). Self-regulation and depletion of limited resources: Does self-control resemble a muscle? *Psychological Bulletin, 126,* 247–259.
44. Baumeister, R. F., & Thierney, J. (2011). *Willpower: Rediscovering the greatest human strength.* Penguin Press HC.
45. Vohs, K. D., Baumeister, R. F., Schmeichel, B. J., Twenge, J. M., Nelson, N. M., & Tice, D. M. (2008). Making choices impairs subsequent self-control: A limited-resource account of decision making, self-regulation, and active initiative. *Journal of Personality and Social Psychology, 94,* 883–898.
46. Steel, P. (2011). *The procrastination equation.* Edingburgh: Pearson Education Limited.
47. Eric Pooley (31 December 2001). 'Mayor of the world.' *Time.* http://www.time.com/time/poy2001/poyprofile.html. Retrieved 5 October 2007.
48. Tykocinski, O. E., & Pittman, T. S. (1998). The consequences of doing nothing: Inaction inertia as avoidance of anticipated counterfactual regret. *Journal of Personality and Social Psychology, 75,* 607–616.
49. Tykocinski, O. E., & Pittman, T. S. (2001). Product aversion following a missed opportunity: Price contrast or avoidance of anticipated regret? *Basic and Applied Social Psychology, 23,* 149–156.
50. Samuelson, W. R., & Zeckhauser, R. J. (1988). Status quo bias in decision making. *Journal of Risk and Uncertainty, 1,* 7–59.
51. Kahneman, D., & Tversky, A. (1979). Prospect theory: An analysis of decisions under risk. *Econometrica, 47,* 263–291.
52. Ritov, I., & Baron, J. (1992). Status quo and omission biases. *Journal of Risk and Uncertainty, 5,* 49–62.
53. Spranca, M. D., Minsk, E., & Baron, J. (1991). Omission and commission in judgment and choice. *Journal of Experimental Social Psychology, 27,* 76–105.
54. Cooper Ramo, Joshua (27 December 1999). 'Jeffrey Preston Bezos: 1999 Person of the year'. *Time Magazine,* http://www.time.com/time/archive/preview/0,10987,992927,00.html.
55. LaGesse, David (19 November 2008). 'America's Best Leaders: Jeff Bezos, Amazon.com CEO'. *U.S. News & World Report,* http://www.usnews.com/articles/news/best-leaders/2008/11/19/americas-best-leaders-jeff-bezos-amazoncom-ceo.html.

References

56. Richburg, Keith B. (15 August 2011). 'Xi Jinping, likely China's next leader, called pragmatic, low-key'. *The Washington Post*, http://www.washingtonpost.com/world/asia-pacific/xi-jinping-likely-chinas-next-leader-called-pragmatic-low-key/2011/08/15/gIQA5W83GJ_story.html.
57. Nijstad, B. A. (2011). *Moeilijke beslissingen*. Universiteit Groningen, Nederland.
58. Nijstad, B. A., & Kaps, S. C. (2008). Taking the easy way out: Preference diversity, decision strategies, and decision refusal in groups. *Journal of Personality and Social Psychology, 94*, 860–870.
59. Judge, T. A., Bono, J. E., Ilies, R., & Gerhardt, M. W. (2002). Personality and leadership: A qualitative and quantitative review. *Journal of Applied Psychology, 87*, 765–780.
60. Berzonsky, A. D., & Ferrari, J. R. (1996). Identity orientation and decisional strategies. *Personality and Individual Differences, 20*, 597–606.
61. Milgram, N., & Tenne, R. (2000). Personality correlates of decisional and task avoidant procrastination. *European Journal of Personality, 14*, 141–156.
62. French President Is Best Dressed Pol, *CBS*, 9 August 2007 (English).
63. Gordon Brown tops GQ worst dressed man poll, *Daily Mirror*, 4 January 2010 (original *GQ* article no longer available).
64. *Philosophie Magazine*, nr 8, April 2007; online extracts.
65. De Dreu, C. K. W., & van de Vliert, E. (1997). *Using conflicts in organizations*. Sage.
66. Avlio, B. J. (2005). Authentic leadership development: Getting to the root of positive forms of leadership. *The Leadership Quarterly*, 315–338.
67. Bazerman, M. H., & Tenbrunsel, A. E. (2011). *Blindspots*. Princeton: Princeton University Press.
68. De Cremer, D. (2012). Leaders need a lesson in crisis management. *Financial Times*, 23 January.
69. Ross, L. (1977). The intuitive psychologist and his shortcomings: Distortions in the attribution process. In L. Berkowitz (Ed.), *Advances in experimental social psychology* (Vol. 10, pp. 173–220). New York: Academic Press.
70. Lerner, J. S., & Tetlock, P. E. (1999). Accounting for the effects of accountability. *Psychological Bulletin, 125*, 255–275.
71. Tetlock, P., Skitka, L., & Boettger, R. (1989). Social and cognitive strategies for coping with accountability: Conformity, complexity and bolstering. *Journal of Personality and Social Psychology, 57*, 632–640.

References

72. Baumeister, R. F., Muraven, M., & Tice, D. M. (2000). Ego depletion: A resource model of volition, self-regulation, and controlled response. *Social Cognition, 18,* 130–150.
73. Rousseau, D. M., Sitkin, S. B., Burt, R. S., & Camerer, C. (1998). Not so different at all: across discipline view of trust. *Academy of Management Review, 23,* 393–404.
74. Dirks, K., & Ferrin, D. (2002). Trust in leadership: Meta-analytic findings and implications for research and practices. *Journal of Applied Psychology, 87,* 611–628.
75. Mayer, R. C., Davis, J. H., & Schoorman, F. D. (1995). An integrative model of organizational trust. *Academy of Management Review, 20,* 709–734.
76. Skowronski, J. J., & Carlston, D. E. (1989). Negativity and extremity biases in impression formation: A review of explanations. *Psychological Bulletin, 105,* 131–142.
77. Whitener, E. M., Brodt, S. E., Korsgaard, A., & Werner, J. M. (1998). Managers as initiators of trust: An exchange relational framework for understanding managerial trustworthy behavior. *Academy of Management Review, 23,* 513–530.
78. De Cremer, D., & Tyler, T. R. (2005). Am I respected or Not? Inclusion and reputation as issues in group membership. *Social Justice Research, 18,* 121–152.
79. Brockner, J., Siegel, P. A., Daly, J. P., Tyler, T. R., & Martin, C. (1997). When trust matters: the moderating effect of outcome favorability. *Administrative Science Quarterly, 42,* 558–583.
80. De Cremer, D. (2012). Controlled wisdom. *Business Strategy Review, 23,* 86–87.
81. Opotow, S. (1990). Moral exclusion and injustice: An introduction. *Journal of Social Issues, 46,* 1–20.
82. Leventhal, G. S. (1980). What should be done with equity theory?: New approaches to the fairness in social relationships. In K. Gergen, M. Greenberg, & R. Willis (Eds.), *Social exchange theory* (pp. 27–55). New York: Plenum.
83. Meindl, J. R. (1995). The romance of leadership as a follower-centric theory: A social constructionist approach. *Leadership Quarterly, 6,* 329–341.
84. Wilson, T. D., & Gilbert, D. T. (2005). Affective forecasting: Knowing what to want. *Current Directions in Psychological Science, 14,* 131–134.
85. Kahneman, D., & Tversky, A. (1979). Prospect theory: An analysis of decisions under risk. *Econometrica, 47,* 263–291.

References

86. Messick, D. M., & Brewer, M. B. (1983). Solving social dilemmas. In L. Wheeler & P. R. Shaver (Eds.), *Review of personality and social psychology* (Vol. 4, pp. 11–44). Beverly Hills: Sage publications.
87. Samuelson, C. D., Messick, D. M., Rutte, C., & Wilke, H. (1984). Individual and structural solutions to resource dilemmas in two cultures. *Journal of Personality and Social Psychology, 47,* 94–104.
88. Hofstede, G. (1983). National cultures in four dimensions: A research-based theory of cultural differences among nations. *International Studies of Management & Organization, 13,* 46–74.
89. Hofstede, G. (1991). *Cultures and organizations: Software of the mind.* McGraw-Hill Book Company (U.K.) Limited: Berkshire, England.
90. Hofstede, G. (1985). The interaction between national and organizational value systems. *Journal of Management Studies, 22,* 347–357.
91. Hofstede, G. (1985). The interaction between national and organizational value systems. *Journal of Management Studies, 22,* 347–357.
92. Chinese Culture Connection (a group of 22 researchers) (1987). Chinese values and the search for culture-free dimensions of culture. *Journal of Cross-Cultural Psychology, 18,* 143–164.
93. Mann, L. (1998). Cross-cultural differences in self-reported decision-making style and confidence. *International Journal of Psychology, 33,* 325–335.
94. Klassen, R. M., Ang, R. P., Chong, W. H., Krawchuk, L. L., Huan, V. S., Wong, I. Y. F., & Yeo, L. S. (2009). A cross-cultural study of adolescent procrastination. *Journal of Research on Adolescence, 19,* 799–811.
95. Ferrari, J. R., Diaz-Morales, J. F., O'Callaghan, J., Diaz, K., & Argumedo, D. (2007). Frequent behavioural delay tendencies by adults: International prevalence rates of chronic procrastination. *Journal of Cross-Cultural Psychology, 38,* 458–464.
96. Reuben, E., Sapienza, P., & Zingales, L. (2008). *Procrastination and impatience.* NBER working paper, Chicago.
97. Steel, P. (2011). *The procrastination equation.* Edingburgh: Pearson Education Limited.
98. Steel, P. (2011). *The procrastination equation.* Edingburgh: Pearson Education Limited.
99. Sirois, F. M., Melia-Gordon, M. L., & Pychyl, T. A. (2003). "I'll look after my health, later": An investigation of procrastination and health. *Personality and Individual Differences, 35,* 1167–1184.
100. Cacioppo, J. T., Hawkley, L. C., Crawford, L. E., Ernst, J. M., Burleson, M. H., Kowalewski, R. B., Malarkey, W. B., Van Cauter, E., &

References

Berntson, G. G. (2002). Loneliness and health: Potential mechanisms. *Psychosomatic Medicine, 64,* 407–17.

101. Martin, T. R., Flett, G. C., Hewitt, P. L., Krames, L., & Szanto, G. (1996). Personality correlates of depression and health symptoms: A test of a self-regulation model. *Journal of Research in Personality, 30,* 264–277.

102. Schweitzer, M. E., Hershey, J. C., & Bradlow, E. T. (2006). Promises and lies: Restoring violated trust. *Organizational Behavior and Human Decision Processes, 101,* 1–19.

103. Folger, R. (1977). Distributive and procedural justice: Combined impact of "voice" and improvement of experienced inequity. *Journal of Personality and Social Psychology, 35,* 108–119.

104. De Cremer, D. (2010). On rebuilding trust. *Business Strategy Review, 21,* 79–80.

105. Van Knippenberg, D., & Hogg, M. A. (2003). A social identity model of leadership effectiveness. In R. T. Kramer & B. M. Staw (Eds.), *Research in organizational Behavior* (Vol. 25, pp. 245–297). Amsterdam: Elsevier.

106. De Cremer, D., van Dijke, M., & Bos, A. E. R. (2007). When leaders are seen as transformational: The effects of organizational justice. *Journal of Applied Social Psychology, 37,* 1797–1816.

107. Judge, T. A., Piccolo, R. F., & Ilies, R. (2004). The forgotten ones? The validity of consideration and initiating structure in leadership research. *Journal of Applied Psychology, 89,* 36–51.

108. Bass, B. M. (1990). *Bass and Stogdill's handbook of leadership.* New York: Free Press.

109. Judge, T. A., Piccolo, R. F., & Ilies, R. (2004). The forgotten ones? The validity of consideration and initiating structure in leadership research. *Journal of Applied Psychology, 89,* 36–51.

110. Kirkpatrick, S. A., Locke, E. A., & Latham, G. P. (1996). Implementing the vision: How is it done? *Polish Psychological Bulletin, 27,* 93–106.

111. Scott, S. G., & Bruce, R. A. (1994). Determinants of innovative behavior: A path model of individual innovation in the workplace. *Academy of Management Journal, 37,* 580–607.

112. Amabile, T. M. (1988). A model of creativity and innovation in organizations. In B. M. Staw & L. L. Cummings (Eds.), *Research in organizational behavior* (Vol. 10, pp. 123–167). Greenwich, JT: JAI Press.

113. De Cremer, D., & van Knippenberg, D. (2004). Charismatic leadership, collective identification, and leadership effectiveness: The interactive

effects of leader self-sacrifice and self-confidence. *Organizational Behavior and Human Decision Processes, 95,* 140–155.
114. Conger, J. A., & Kanungo, R. N. (1998). *Charismatic leadership in organizations.* Thousand Oaks, CA: Sage.
115. Isaac, W. (2012). The real leadership lessons of Steve Jobs. *Harvard Business Review, April,* 93–102.
116. Maak, T. (2007). Responsible leadership, stakeholder engagement, and the emergence of social capital. *Journal of Business Ethics, 74,* 329–343.
117. Avolio, B. J., & Gardner, W. L. (2005). Authentic leadership development: Getting to the root of positive forms of leadership. *Leadership Quarterly, 16,* 315–338.
118. Lord, R. G., & Hall, R. J. (2005). Identity, deep structure and the development of leadership skill. *Leadership Quarterly, 16,* 591–615.
119. Chu, A. H. C., & J. N. Choi. 2005. Rethinking procrastination: Positive effects of "active" procrastination behavior on attitudes and performance. *Journal of Social Psychology, 14,* 245–264.
120. Bluedron, A. C., & Denhardt, R. B. (1988). Time and organizations. *Journal of Management, 14,* 299–320.
121. Gunia, B., Wang, L., Huang, L., Wang, J., & Murnighan, J. K. (2012). Contemplation and conversation: Subtle influences on moral decision making. *Academy of Management Journal, 55,* 13–33.
122. Snyder, M., & Cantor, N. (1998). Understanding personality and social behavior: A functionalist strategy. In D. Gilbert, S. Fiske, & G. Lindzey (Eds.), *Handbook of social psychology* (Vol. 1, pp. 635–679). New York: McGraw-Hill.
123. Watkins, M. D. (2012). How managers become leaders. *Harvard Business Review,* June, 65–71.
124. DeRue, D. S., Nahrgan, J. D., Hollenbeck, J. R., & Workman, K. (2012). A quasi-experimental study of after-event reviews and leadership development. *Journal of Applied Psychology, 97,* 997–1015.

Index

Note: Locators followed by '*f*' and '*t*' refer to figures and tables.

absence of competence, 57
absence of trust, *see* distrust
action orientation, 25
active leadership, 13
after-events reviews, 106
alcoholism, 88
alternatives, 37–9
   attractive, 38
   choices, 38*f*
   differentiation level, 37
   features of, 37
   postponement, 37
alternatives, unattractive, 39
anonymity, 53–6
   absence of, 55
   challenges, 56*t*
   conflict of interests, 54
   element of responsibility, 53
   lack of, 55
   position of authority, 53
anticipated emotion, 24
   see also emotion regulation
assumptions about leadership, 12–3
9/11 attack, 8, 29
authenticity, 47–51
   art of, 49
   concept of, 48
   decision–consequences correlation, 48
   insecurity and uncertainty, 49
   internal contradiction, 49
   key themes, 48
   strengths and weaknesses, 48–9
   traps, 50
authentic leadership, 49, 107

Banerjee, Mamata, 51
behavioural accounting, 9
behavioural approach, 11–2
behavioural consistency, 59
behavioural decision-making, 9
behavioural economics, 9, 18
behavioural finance, 9
behavioural integrity, 59
behavioural psychology, 18
behavioural tradition, 10
blindspots, 50
breach of trust, 91
bureaucratic approach, 66

Cameron, David, 51
Clinton, Bill, 1
Clinton, Hillary Rodham, 63–4
cohesion and social affiliations, 12
collectivistic cultures, 83
conceptual understanding, 15–6
conflict avoidance, 45–7
   conflict anticipation, 46
   constructive opening, 46
   damage of mutual relations, 45
   escalation, 45
   fear of, 45
   openness, 46
   transparency, 46

Confucian dynamism, 76–7, 81–2
  cultural dimension, 81
  ethical decisions, 82
  limited anonymity, 82
  variables, 82
consequences of decisions, 113–14
constructive opening, 46
Cook, Tim, 72
corrective feedback, 32
counterfactual thinking, 30
Cremer, David De, 115
cross-cultural differences, 84

decision–consequences correlation, 48
decision dilemma, 33
decision-making, decentralised, 4
  implementation and, 18
  individual variables, 19*t*
  legitimacy of, 9
  management of, 31
  threshold for, 49
decision process theory, 6
decisions, 5–7
  crucial element of effective leadership, 5
  path-goal theory, 6
decisions postponing, *see* procrastination
delaying decisions, 15, 18, 76, 83, 85, 90, 92, 95–8, 102, 105, 108
  negative consequences, 14
  pitfalls, 14
  pivotal role of decision-making, 15
  understanding, 14
  consequences
    alcoholism, 88
    breach of trust, 91
    conflicts, 88
    depression, 89

    financial, 85–7
    health, 87–9
    mutual trust, 91
    polarisation of opinions, 88
    procrastinating behaviour, 86
    psychological contracts, 91
    social consequences, 90*f*
  how of, 102–5
    intrinsic influences, 102
  why of, 105–7
    dimensions, 105–6
    individual characteristics, 105
    situational characteristics, 105
democratic leader, 7–9
  characterise, 9
  democratic values, 8
  effective decision-making, 7
  prescription, 7
  process element, 8
depression, 89
d'Equainville, David, 2
devil's advocate, 28*t*
dictatorship, 66
distraction, 20
distrust, 56–61
  actions, 59
  behavioural consistency, 59
  behavioural integrity, 59
  benevolence, 59
  challenge of trust building, 58*t*
  communication with followers, 60
  competence, 59
  dimensions, 59
  influence on the decision-making process, 58
  integrity, 59
  relation with followers, 60
  sense of control, 60
Dutch polder model, 66

Index

ego-depletion, 55
emotion regulation, 24–30
   action orientation, 25
   fear of regret, 24
   postponing of decisions, 24
   self-control, 26
   self-image, 25–6
equality, principle of, 66
ethical decisions, 64–7
   anticipatory approach, 65
   bureaucratic approach, 66
   challenges of, 67–8*t*
   essence of ethics, 65
   focus on, 65
   morality, 64–5
   moral principle, 64, 66
   realistic ethical evaluation, 66
   social power, 64
   subjective interpretation, 65
   trial-and-error, 65
Eurocrisis, 4, 33
exhaustion, physical and mental, 111–12
exploitation, 56
extrinsic influences, 104

false feeling of control, 26, 61
Ferrari, Joseph, 84
financial crisis, 18, 33
freedom, principles of, 66
furious' leader, 42
future predictions, 35

gender difference, 84
Giuliani, Rudolph, 8, 29
global leadership
   avoiding conflicts, 78
   Confucian dynamism, 81–2
   cultural differences, 77
   cultural dimension, 77*t*

   cultural typology, 76
   cultures, 80
   dimensions, 76
   distrust, 78
   individualism, 79–80
   masculinity, 80–1
   neuroticism, 80
   power distance, 77–8
   status quo, 79
   sub-optimal decisions, 80
   uncertainty avoidance, 78–9
Greece, Eurocrisis, 4

Herculean task, 4
high expectations, 41, 51, 107
high-expectations leaders, 41
Histories, 32
Hofstede, Geert, 76
Hollande, François, 39

illusion of control, 61–3
'I love myself' leader, 42–3
immobilisation, 21
inaction inertia, 30–2
incompetence, social image, 54
indecisiveness, 9, 21, 23
   negative consequences and, 23
individualism, 76, 79–80
interactive approach, 9
interactive model, 101*f*
intrinsic motivations, 98
irrational behaviour, 9, 10*f*, 11, 19–20, 24, 37, 61, 97, 100
irrational human nature, 35
irrelevant distractions, 27

Jinping, Xi, 36
Jobs, Steve, 94
Johnson, Boris, 29–30

laissez-faire leadership, 2
leader–follower relationship, 97

Index

leaderless teams, 4
leader, perspective of, 1
leadership, definition, 3*t*, 6
Leadership on Hold (survey), 115–19
   context, 118–19
   individual, 116–17
logical feedback, 60

masculinity, 76, 80–1, 84
   definition, 80
   lack of previous success, 81
   new leader, 81
   regulation of emotions, 81
   variables, 81
my responsibilities, idea of, 67

negative emotions, 24
   see also emotion regulation
negative feedback, 107
Netanyahu, Benjamin, 47
neuroticism, 39–45
   charisma, 43
   decision avoidance, 40
   fear of self-evaluation, 44
   furious' leader, 42
   high-expectations leaders, 41
   high levels, 40
   I love myself leader, 42–3
   negative correlation, 40
   procrastination, 40
   types, 41
   unpredictable leader, 43–4
neurotic leadership, characteristic of, 79
new leader, 68–72
   challenges, 69*t*
   competence, 69, 71
   consequences, 69
   elements, 71–2

misconceptions, 68
relationships with others, 70
social challenge, 69
Nijstad, Bernard, 37
non-anonymous situations, 55

Obama, Barack, 5, 10, 61, 64
The Odyssey, 27–8
onion effect, 18–9
openmindedness, 57
over-optimistic tendency, 19

path-goal theory, 6
Paul, Ronald, 51
people orientation, 46
perceptions, positive leadership, 93*t*
personal characteristics, consequence of, 52
personal intuition, 11
personality of leader, 19, 104
planning fallacy, 22
   see also procrastination
political euphemism, 40
poor management of emotions, 31
positive leadership perceptions, 93–7
   action-driven approach, 94
   authenticity, 96–7
   communication strategy, 96
   competence, 94
   delaying decisions, 95
   legitimacy of, 95
   responsibility, 96
   social affiliations, 93
   strategy, 95–6
   transparent culture, 95
   vision, 93
postponement of decision, 40
power distance, 76–8, 84
Preston, Jeffrey, 36

Index

previous success, lack of, 72–5
  common reaction, 73
  decisions postponement, 72
  failure and uncertainty, 74
  negative experience, impact of, 72
  optimism, 74–5
  realistic possibility, 74
  take-aways for dealing, 73*t*
proactive leadership, 13–4
problems identification, 1
procrastinating behaviour, 10, 17, 23, 30, 40, 48, 53, 57, 62, 86–7, 89, 91–2, 106, 109, 111
procrastination
  alcoholism, 88
  bad and good of, 99*t*
  commonly used 'reasons,' 21
  constructive approach, 98
  criteria, 20
  cross-cultural differences, 83
  cultural differences, 77, 84
  decision-making problem, 97
  delaying tasks, 97
  effortlessness, 21
  emotional level, 23
  factors, 100
  global leadership and, 76
  ill health and, 89
  incorrect assessment of time, 21
  levels of, 104–5
  male vs. female, 84
  masters of self-deception, 21
  perceptions and, 92
  principles to beat, 109*t*
  relation with time, 22
  self-serving goals, 98
  stress and, 87
  tendency to overestimate, 22
  tried-and-tested abilities, 23
  uncertainty, 61

rational approach, 18
rational control of emotions, 8
regret emotion, 31

sabotage, *see* procrastination
Sandberg, Sheryl, 63
Sarkozy, Nicolas, 39, 44–5
self-analysis, 41
self-assessment, 49
self-control, 23, 26–7, 43, 55, 82, 84, 86, 101, 103
self-deception, 19, 21, 26
self-image, 25–6, 49, 55, 73, 101, 106
self-opinionated attitude, 44
self-regulation, inefficient forms, 102–3
sense of control, 42, 60
situational awareness, 53
social feedback, 54
social glue, 56
social pressure, 9, 54–6, 105
social situation, influence of, 52
status quo, 33–6
  future predictions, 35
  irrational human nature, 35
  meaning, 33
  presence of, 34
Steel, Piers, 27, 86
strategic level, 24

task details to a leader, 103–4
  catalyst of change, 104
  generalist, 103
  integrator, 103–4
task orientation, 46
time perceptions, 82–3
  industrialisation, 83
  procrastination and, 83
  time–efficiency schedules, 83

transformational leadership
 theory, 7
Truman, Harry S., 6
trust building, 58*t*

uncertainties elimination, 110–11
uncertainty avoidance, 76, 78–9
 define, 78–9
 neuroticism, 79
 status quo, 79
uncertainty, 61–4
 circumstances, 62–3
 coping with, 63
 decisions postponing, 62
 procrastination, 61
unpredictable leader, 43–4

Walker, Scott, 67
well-considered decisions, 32
work at relationship, 112–13

Yang, Wang, 60